INSIDE OUT HEART
Collection

Volumes 1 & 2

Poems for my dying father & after

Diary notes of being with dying father

SJP Dooley

INSIDE OUT HEART

Volume 1: Poems for my dying father & after

SJP Dooley

Copyright © 2020 by SJP Dooley

All rights reserved.

No part of this book may be reproduced in any form or any means, including information storage and retrieval systems, without the author's written permission, except brief quotations in a book review.

Volumes 1 & 2 Collection

Ebook ISBN: 978-1-922399-07-6

Paperback ISBN: 978-1-922399-06-9

Audiobook ISBN: 978-1-922399-08-3

www.stellarviolets.org

 A catalogue record for this work is available from the National Library of Australia

 Published by Stellar Violets

For Peter Stanley Lees Dooley

&

for all of us who are living with dying

FOREWORD & POEM BY NIEL VAUGHAN

Poetry, for me, is a spiritual experience.

It never fails to astonish when something so complex and ethereal comes through the fingers and onto the page alive and fully formed.

It's a process of feelings and reactions.

I take a drink to invoke the spirits. Find a comfy couch and then begin to read you, your history, your poetry, your inner world. It's intimate and sad in that delightful way we enjoy Greek tragedies.

When my eyes begin to swim it's time for a dip in the subconscious; cool moss underfoot as the shadow self enters the inner deep;

. . .

the inner self detaches from the senses; a flash of lightning on the horizon; then, the rumble shudders and your poem arrives.

Witness the Witness

His father is preparing for what's coming next
  while he channels the path into text

The son witnessing the father slipping in-between
  into the place no living eye has ever seen

The brutal order of the living process
  a well-worn hand leaving his face with a gentle caress

And in these pages that follow
  lies a charted path into a dawning tomorrow

  For Simon

Niel Vaughan, Castlemaine 2020

THE ORIGINAL FALLEN GIANT
(FACING THIS ALONE)

A giant has fallen across my path
and now I don't know how to get through,
or what to do,
so I write this,
moved to irrelevance
as I contemplate
the size and force of this monolithic impediment.
And, so I begin to crawl across,
to go over and continue along the path.
But the grunting sounds repel me
beneath the giant,
back down the track,
down,
deeper into the forest.

Words

Words are useful, but only when nothing else will suffice.

IN WE LOVE MARGARET RESERVE

In We Love Margaret Reserve
We are supported
By a chair
And warm blanket to
Comfort you
From the biting cold
As you ease yourself
Into your chair
Bathe in warm sun's rays
Blinding even
Take the fruit
And
breakfast upon it
To help you on your long day's journey
Take some more
You'll need it Son
And, yes
It's like a treasure trove
For you

A playground
As you know
As he said
You're not alone
We are supported
This is home
I call to you
I love you Son
You know that
Tears
For each one
Don't let this go
You know
This rock
He has supported
But needs your help
We are supported
In this place
Allow yourself
Release the pace
Allow yourself
Feel the space
Allow yourself
Heart's embrace
Allow yourself
Sweet the taste
You have the time
Now look around
Come over here
Hear the sound
Of this bee
Coming for me
Sweet scent of rose

Of being home
Allow yourself
To feel this place
This my Son
My love's embrace

LATER IN WE LOVE MARGARET RESERVE

Later in We Love Margaret Reserve
This water backed up
(Possibly for years)
Comes forth
At first a trickle
Rivulets flow
Moisture
Staining the barren rock
Filtered by sand
Wind whipping leaves
The tempest builds
This water
Having now emerged from the depths
Reflects this Sun
Shimmers in this wind
Mirrors this place
Like a dog gnawing a boney stick
And running
In circles
Impossible to apprehend

You released this water
You did this
You always could
You just
Did not know it
Now you know
Pick up your stick
Your bone
And go
Run
Run
You cannot be caught
You are that wind
And you are running
And cannot be apprehended

LAND OF FORGOTTEN DREAMING

I'm letting the land wash over me
as we press on.
Ever onward
into this land of forgotten dreaming.
Images,
real,
come forth unbidden.
Passing out of sight before comprehension.
A calf rises to her mother's call.
The track,
fenced off.
Impassable.
A tiny track
spearing off.
Intimidating,
cutting off,
verging out,
and merging in.

2 FLIES CAUGHT IN A WEB

2 flies caught in a web
A larger blacker form emerges
Grabs one
A ferocious buzzing
It's still alive
Scooped up
Bundled
Rapidly carried into the lair
Stillness
Until the second fly moves
A larger blacker form swoops
And they are gone

CAGE-STRUCK

I am stuck
Inside this cage
Terrified
I screech
And flap
Interred
Within this trap
While you
My love
Flap
Like a mirror
Before me
And you are seen
And I am heard
The helper comes
To get me out
I flap and screech
His calm hands enveloping
I am whisked into the light

Freedom
Reunited
We fly to the highest branch

NUYTSIA FLORIBUNDA

Nuytsia floribunda are out.
WA Xmas trees.
Pangs of regret at leaving this place, at this time, for so long.
What am I doing?
And why?
I'm going to see Nicola and it is worth it.
It's a long trip.
Wondering whether Dad will ever see WA again?
Perhaps not...
What is going on?
I don't know.
The light blue sky and bright light is all pervasive.
Everything is so bright and tinged with a yellow hue.

GARETH

The gate fixed shut
when finally I arrive.
Wrenching, struggling,
sneaking beneath creepers,
crushed geranium wafting.
Crashing
onto my path
after all this time.
The youthful old gum
whose trunk stained with tears
now reflects this Summer's Sun.
And I am home
upon this path
after years.
Cutting meaninglessly
along the gumboot creek,
we walk that path forever
Gareth.

UNUSED TICKET

*He's unlikely to return
to this bush
he owns
but never really walked,
preferring roses
and lawn.
Dried branches snap.
He loved his view.
He loves his view.
Everyone does.
But I am taken
here.
Past the sewerage pipe.
Down,
down,
the mysterious
bubbling,
and holes for snakes.
The mystery sounds.*

Unseen
I know it.

FOREST SENTINEL

A rainbow
In the forest
Sentinel
Maintains this place
For us
Our feathers yet wet
Looking out
Readying ourselves
For the time to fly

ONE SQUARE FOOT

On this one square foot
    On which I stand
    I am
    Completely
    Here
    And
    Memories
    Exist
    But
    Do not
    Hold me
    Alone
    I walk
    Aware
    I walk
    Knowing
    I walk
    Standing
    I stand

Knowing
I stand

4:39AM (ON THE FIRST DAY OF YOUR LAST YEAR ON EARTH)

I like to feel the cold embrace of the morning air
As it freshens and wakens me
Calling forth a new day
A new year even
Cool
Refreshing
Beckoning
Calming
Soothing
Healing
Rewarding
Enabling
Beginning
Anew

THOSE TOO HEAVY SOUNDS

The ocean is so loud in my left ear
I can hardly hear myself think.
The right feels like an open vacuum with birds occasionally calling.
That sound of the ocean rumbling like that and crashing so loud in my left ear,
while my right ear is shielded from that.
Those too heavy sounds are not peaceful.
They are loud and overbearing,
but the soft sand is so soft,
and the soft water is sweet to my feet.
And so
I continue walking along this shore
in spite of that raucous sound.

HELD BY YOU (3RD AND FINAL OP)

Blue
Iridescent
Welcome
You hold me
I am you
Resting on the flexing bough
By the trickling stream
Far from the traffic
In this our home
Floating free
You welcome me
Here
In your ease calming
Holding me
In arrest
As darkness descends
Your iridescence continues to shine
You are not swayed by this night
You are the blue butterfly
Home

In this Jurassic world
Where nothing can retain you
An embodied spirit of this place
We hold each other
Free
Together
We are both transformed
Free together
We rise and fall
Free together
We sit
And listen
Trickling stream
Caws of crows
Cicadas a ton
Rumbling plane
And we sit
Together
We are free
And I am so grateful for our meeting
I walk on with you
Together
In freedom
Thank you
And
Goodnight

LIQUID HEART

Night scents fill the air
White petals fall
The last remaining rose of summer
Into the darkness I walk alone
Shining lights behind me
Darkness fills my vision
My heart liquid
I walk
Into the night

AT ALICE ROBINSON RESERVE 2 APRIL

Dad and Lucy came here all the time.
And Mum lived there.
Now they are all gone and only we are left.
And yet I can still see Nicola and Dad and Lucy there at the swings and the seats.
But that time has gone.
And only I am left.
Nicola is with her boyfriend, Pat.
And Dad is struggling with many things including his loneliness, at Gracewood Retirement Village.
And it's all painful.
And sorrowful.
And hard work.
And such loss.
Such loss.
Dad, who so easily walked up to this small park, will no longer be walking up here again.
And it's so sad and upsetting.
And I really don't know what to do.
Because there isn't anything I can do.

It is all past.

So I stop, and I smell the white rose at Jim the Roseman's place, the one that gives me the feeling of drinking fresh lemonade.

"A monarch butterfly *came and just lightly touched my heart and flittered away*"

LAND OF SADNESS, LONGING

There's something so sad about this landscape
So dry
So barren
So wasted
Such a wasteland
Waterless
It's marked by water
Absent of colour
It emphasises the blue sky
Sepia toned ink blots
Dried
Empty
Rectilinear
Sun faded
Bleached
A faded, colourless
Flat expanse
With oval salt pans

FLYING BACK TO DAD

Lights glimmer,
dazzling
as our torch rises
yet again.
Again, and again, and again.
In awe,
in wonder.
Airport waking up,
turbines whirring,
daylight emerging.
People mobbing
to this place
of arrivals
& departures.
The one celebrated,
the other mourned
in these tough times,
as they've always been.
Airbus A330 – 200

clomping like cloven hooves
our Virgin
Aircrew herd along the hard tiles;
"How's your Mum?"
"Yeah she's good."
Looks like it'll be the emptiest flight since 23 January & I
remember 2 years ago when
things were different
and
Dad was undiagnosed.
April 2017
& Nic & Carolyn shut down & I
Couldn't get Nic
& Dad, who was well then, & I
drove around
Galston
trying to get Nic
unsuccessfully,
& in 2 years time
he will have been gone some time
& that's
unbearably sad
as the night
is gone
and
heralded by
pink, blue
pastel hues
morning is
ours.
Korean Air with a Pepsi logo.
Jetstar
& our A330 – 200

awaiting.
Being packed &
readied.
Are we ever ready?
I am here for you Nic, just as Pa
has been for me!

TO BE AWARE

The idea is to be aware.
Painfully, and,
Ruthlessly
AWARE!
Living fully
Through the senses.
Experiencing it all.
Being & remaining
Open.
To experience.
To truth.
To connection.
She.
Her.
Her.
She moves me
In ways I have
Never understood,
But that my mother
Had an inkling of.

I continue to be moved
& confused & bewildered
& hurt & upset &
Embarrassed & opened
Up.
I feel the river of life
Lifting me
Up & off the
Muddy surface
& racing me
Along within
Its torrent
Bumping, colliding
With others in
Life & then away again.

DRIVING

One of my enduring memories of Dad, is of him driving.
Driving,
Always driving.
Driving our family,
Like Clark Griswold,
On trips
Up and down
The coast & to
Queensland.
Driving us in the
Dark
As I sat in the back dreaming
Of the girl I loved,
Listening to Go West's
The King of Wishful Thinking,
Or
Was it,
We Close Our Eyes?
As he drove himself &
His 3 sons

For a hospital visit
To his wife at
St John of God, Richmond.
Or
Was it
Windsor, or Richmond?
He loved driving &
Had many stories of
Driving old Austin A40s
Without windscreen
Wipers or heaters.

SOMEWHERE

Somewhere over the
Southern Ocean
The white caps
Of that frigid
Sea
Whip up
Beneath the sunny
Blue sky

I ASK THE BIRDS IN THE SKY, "HOW AM I GOING TO COPE WITH ALL OF THIS?"

How am I going to cope with all of this?

I'm asking you for help Gareth,
asking for help from the universe.

Asking for help from the spirits,
from everybody,
from friends,
from family,
from animals and plants,
from the sticks and stones,
from all there is,
in the trees,
in the sky,
and the sun, especially the sun,
and all of the beings, unseen and alive.

Find the joy, find the joy, find the joy.

Sit with the pain.

Walk, walk, walk.

Murmuration of the birds,
murmuration of the birds,
these birds
coming into the light,
into the light,
into the light,
into the black,
then the white,
and then turning back,
turning above me,
white birds fluttering,
fluttering, fluttering,
then black birds,
and white again,
and then gone.

Only to return again on the next circling.

Circling birds
catching the morning light.
Circling birds catching the morning sun.
Birds.
Birds.
40 or more birds circling together as one.
Free within the space of space.
As one they become dark and continue to circle, and as they circle
as one they become white against blue sky
as they continue to circle.
They continue to circle into the light,
and into the dark,
into the light,

and into the dark,
into the light again,
a circling manifestation of existence
into the light,
circling into the dark,
circling into the light,
circling in the dark
always beautiful,
always in motion,
always Life.
And they have no great awareness
of their circling into the light,
and into the dark,
into the light,
and into the dark.

They simply are.

The birds.
The birds circling into the light,
and into the dark,
into the light,
into the dark.
I see them circling
and circling
in continual momentum
as the birds circle
into the light,
into the dark,
and into the light,
and into the dark,
and into the light,
into the dark,

the birds in the sky.

OVER ROOKWOOD

Previously Dad's death was a theoretical eventuality.
Now it is a pressing imminent reality.
It's emotional and somber.
This trip
of ascension.
Remembering that Icarus flew too close to the Sun.
Out of balance.
Fly,
and be aware.
We flew over Rookwood cemetery.
I miss Jervis trips with Nic.
The beauty of the snaking river astounds me.
It slowly expands out to a lake.
It is organic.
Its fissures like ink on blotting paper
disappearing into the mist.
It is
so lovely.
I miss it

even as I'm taken
by the blue sky.

HIS PAIN

I can't think straight in here
It's driving me insane
Draining the blood from my bones
Let me out of here
Let me go
Let me outta my Kellyville cage
But no
I remain
Trapped
And alone

DEAR ROSE

Part I

Dear rose
We have travelled
So far
To weep
Together
Dear rose
Intoxicant
That your perfume is
I
Can not inhale enough of you
Nuzzled in
To you
Only song birds witness
Our coming together
And even they do not know

Part II

And so
At the end of it all
I return to you dear rose
Your scent ever same
Even as your flowers shift and age
And wither
Only to be replaced
By new shoots
And flowers
Your scent unwavering
Calling forth
For more

DAD IS DYING

Dad is dying
He has no will to live
Consider this
His life
Ending
Over
Going
From this body that is failing him
Just as he has been failed
Allow him
Space
Be there
Find your own peace
Find your own zen and be that

BEING RELEASED

I have to see this as you being released
Simply released
Naught else
Simply seeing you released
Anything else is not correct
An illusion

MIRROR NOIR

Waking up in the darkness
Mysterious
Black window
Like a black mirror
Revealing nothing
Though everything is there

THE CANAL'S EDGE

Just past the bridge where the muddied bike lays,
there's a path that disappears
where the holly grows,
but if you keep walking, one step after the other will
     take you down stairs to a jetty
whereupon you will gaze
at the mother and her ducklings and listen to the
     sounds of the morning birds
and the passing tram bell.
This is what you will do when your father is dying
and you've done all you can.

THE TRUTH

Dad's body is failing him now.
It happens to all of us.
It's an unbearably bitter pill to swallow.
And we choke, and gag on it.
But the truth is that his body is no longer the capable
  vehicle that it's been for him all his life, that has
  faithfully served him in so many ways
and, so, he is to be released.
Released from his pain and suffering.
And we mourn his pain,
and his loss,
and our loss.
But we are comforted to know that he had a good life.
That he needed relief,
and the relief he needed was granted him.
This is a comfort,
his finding peace.

UNTIL NOW

Burnished glow
Rippling toward me
Just as she came
Once
And visited me
Here
As you did
We did
Together
Countless times
But never stopping
Until
Now

NEW FORMS

These shells are new.
Formed in recent years.
They're made up of stuff;
sand, and aggregates
that were here when I used to come here.
But they are new.
New forms.
And that is the thing
with this death thing.
Yes, the old forms go
but new forms come.
And are the new not beautiful too?

REVEALING GLORY

And there they are again.
The flock of light and shade birds,
as they flutter into the light reflecting whiteness.

Shining bright,

then shifting, turning away from the light.

Becoming shadows of themselves.

Dark and stark against the brightness of the morning sky.

The light and the dark in the one.

The one in the many.

The many forming the one,

but not taking away from

the individuality of the one within the many.

But it is the many that reveal the glory of the flock.

GO

Go.
Let it all go.
Don't waste another moment on any of it.
Relax.

Be.

Feel yourself breathing.
Your blood flowing effortlessly.

You are in this moment, walking on this land that is supporting you.

This is enough.

Continue in joy.

Be cool.

Be whole.

Be whole.

Be whole.
Be whole.
Be whole.
Be whole.

You are within the whole.

Relax.
Go with it.

Look around and see.

And you will see that you lie within your form, and you will see all the forms around you, and you will see all of the forms around you of which your body is one.

And it is nothing to hold onto it, so let it go.

Feel your breath inside you, as your comet is inside you, all good and whole and healthy.

Traumatic moments come and go and you continue on.

Your Comet continues on.

Your Comet continues on.

See you later, and let it go.

Feel it and let it go.

Feel it and let it go.

The past is but a phantom seen, created by your imagination, that never was, and never will be, so let it go and exist within your eternal space now.

Live now.

You are wild.

You are wild happening to be only you,

And,

Live you now.

Live now.

You are alive now.

Put your invitations out without expectation, and simply continue to live.

Be what happens to you now.

There is nothing more to strive for, there is nothing more to gain.

You are living with you, so please leave them.
They are all fine.

Dad is filled with peace, and harmony, and goodness.

You are living now, and the more you let it all go, and live well, the more you will find that all is peace and love and goodness.

CLIMBING MT COUGAL

Climbing Mt Cougal.

Trekking briskly the whole time
right along the edge of the NSW and Qld border
with a barbed wire fence next to me.

Something about this metaphor.

Climbing, climbing.

The only thing harder
than the heart thumping challenge of climbing up
is the slippery, life and limb risking

descent.

SITTING NEXT TO MY FATHER

Sitting next to my father as he quietly lays there peacefully dozing, I wonder;

"What is all this?"

"What is a life?"

"What is life?"

And I can't grasp any of it.

I am not peaceful as he appears to be.

I am confused, and forced into a strained grasping at something that maybe is there, but is not of my present capacity to comprehend.

Perhaps we have everything back to front, and upside down.

Or perhaps it all just is, and we are part of it as is.

It's very lonely, and some other word I can't find to express the feelings/emotions, but it's something of emptiness like a small ship in the night sitting precariously on a vast endless ocean.

PINK BALLOON

A lone pink balloon bounces
away
off the sidewalk
and
into the path of the six lane highway.

It bounces,
and floats,
and is oblivious to
its imminent destruction,
and yet it continues to pop,
and bounce,
and float
and

never dies.

AND AS IT FADES FROM VIEW

*And as it fades from view
I signal to you
my forgiveness
and love*

*You gave me so much
I cannot recall
Everything*

Yet I know that it was good

*And there has been such pain
Amidst the beauty*

*For although I did not show it
I felt it all*

*And I loved it
And that is why it has been so hard
to go*

WE LEAVE THIS WORLD TO OTHERS

We leave this world to others
We leave this world to others
We leave this world to others

Whether we like it or not

We leave this world to others
We leave this world to others
We leave this world to others

Whether we like it or not

We leave this world to others
We leave this world to others

Leave this world to others

Whether you like it or not
everything you have ever loved, owned,

or desired
will be left to others

SOMETIMES

Sometimes it's just so painful

The past

The memories

The pain

I feel it in my gut...

and I wince.

FRAYED

*My nerves are quite frayed around the edges from
    everything*

But I continue on

I don't really have any choice

*I look out over the beauteous cover of Jim the
    Roseman's roses and I am in awe*

And yet there is a pain in the pit of my stomach

We continue to press on

We have no choice

*Dad continues to suffer like nobody else
and that's the worst of it*

IN IT

When you're that close to someone, you're in it

There's no objectifying or anything then

There just is

You're in it,

and that's that

WHEN WAS THE LAST TIME

When was the last time we came up here for a game of cricket?

We didn't know it was going to be the last time,

but it was

the last time.

You,

standing there,

upright.

No miracle then.

It would be now.

Our last game of cricket.

Your last game of cricket.

Who knew?

We didn't.

Best we didn't.

We just enjoyed it.

Our last game of cricket.

Just like your last trip to the park with Lucy.

Lucy's passing, a forerunner to yours.

Bookended by B.

Oh how you would love to be back in those days.

Playing cricket.

Walking Lucy.

Being with B.

And that's where the pain comes.

Knowing what you would love.

And cannot have.

Ever again.

2 STONES GRINDING (TOGETHER)

2 old stones fallen from this mountain

grind hard.

The sound

of pure pain,

of loss beyond what can be spoken.

Intercontinental tectons,

weight dragging

you

from her,

as you

founder,

gasping.

She sits

reading.

She knows

your death,

even as this

breath,

gurgling,

keeps you

from your grave.

That sound

of a moraine

in creation

carves apart this love

to dust.

As, grinding,

stone upon stone,

nothing left,

not even bones,

ground down

ashes, rust,

leaving form,

becoming

us.

FINAL CALL

Undeserving of the pity

Undeserving of the grace

Just let me to sit a while

Taking in this place

Sitting by your bedside

Only at the end

The boat capsized

The captain drowned

Our ship awash with grief

Rapidly descending

*We hear the final call
Letting go the tether*

The snapping of the cord

AHH BUT DO NOT BE NAIVE

Ahh but do not be naive my dear Niel,

This traveller knows a few secrets.

The pain is concomitant with the pleasure.

The joy emerges from the seeds of sorrow.

What we do for others we do for ourselves.

Those who choose not to go will never see the entry sign.

DESCENT

At the counter this morning

Love greets me by name

Mary enquires

How am I today

I tell her the truth

Not easy to bear

Sitting, receptive

She's had worse to bear

She's carried it softly

From Syria here

And now she and Love

At the counter of care

She raises her hand

Betoking a gift

Her hand brings forth

The blessing I need

And as I depart from the counter of Love

I am blessed

While descending

the cool, dark

from above

HE WON'T BE LOOKING AT ANY OF THIS AGAIN

He won't be looking at any of this again from in that body.

It's tough,

And we will miss him and his ways.

We are all struggling.

He's done so well.

In those words of Paul in the bible;

"I have run the race,

I have fought the good fight."

Was that in Corinthians?

SATURDAY 14 DECEMBER

Awaking in the night

Standing

Encompassed by stars

Thinking of those who have passed

TOGETHER (EULOGY FOR DAD)

On the land where I live
a giant tree has fallen across the path.
It is huge. Way too big for any chainsaw.
What to do?
I can't go back,
but confronting its sheer immensity
it feels too much.
But the only way,
the ONLY way
is together.
To take the hand of my travelling companion,
and,
together,
to continue our journey.
Where once this giant stood
strong, and proud, and beautiful,
for years before we came here.
Now
We MUST
face this challenge,

and, in the aftermath
of this giant's death,
a gaping hole left in the forest,
new sunlight lighting our path,
we MUST
grasp this old giant's branches,
and together,
pushing and pulling each other,
climb upon this old giant.
This old giant becoming part of our path,
as he always was, as he sheltered us.
Now, having fallen
somehow touching us more intimately,
as parts of this old giant rub off on our hands, our boots.
As our hands, and knees, and shins are scraped, and out our
blood pours, merges with the crystalline sap of this old giant.
We have never been so close
as in this time, when the giant has fallen
into our hands.

DEATH

Death
It comes in and smashes everything

Incoming tide
Wipes clear all marks

Brickies trowel
Clean slate

Fucking hell
Bam!

All gone
All gone
All gone

47°C
ON 31 DECEMBER

It's so hot my eyes sting

I can feel the heat from the blasting wind peeling the skin off my face

It's ugly heat
Everything is hot to the touch

The car's outside temperature gauge reads 47°C

It's beyond sweat hot

FOR AULD LANG SYNE, MY DEAR

The time keeps passing.

We are in the last day, of the last year with Dad in his body.

And so, in some ways, to let go of this year is to let go of the time with Dad.

And letting go of the time with Dad is not easy.

So letting go of this year is hard.

This new year is our first year without having him the way that we had him for what seems like forever, and in some ways was.

But as the poet said:

"no one can stop time's unfolding.
Never let go of the thread."[1]

END OF THE DYING YEAR

The year ends

In a dry creek bed.

I find myself

Stationary.

Held within cicada force fields,

Burnt umber and sepia tones.

The rock, splintered.

Bitten, scratched and aching

I take the next step.

This year's bark

The ground that I now crunch.

I know the butterfly is here

Although I cannot see her.

And what hurts more,

She knows

But does not reveal.

Walking alone,

Fresh new shoots where the trunk came down.

And I have not been here

Since before this collapse.

And I am the tree.

And the shoots,

And it hurts,

As my fresh bark is exposed to 47 degree days.

The furnace burns all away,

Or almost,

For I remain.

Bereft.

HALF MOON

Half moon above

Half moon below

You struggled so hard

Ascent or decline

Your struggle

Valiant

As you climbed

Your feet dragging

Held by a thread

Diminishing

Struggling

From the bed

Collapsing

Slow motion

Gradually gone

Half moon

Becoming

Moon

Now gone

BROKEN BY THE TREE

So I leapt on that big old tree.

and I slipped,

and it threw me.

And as I lay on the ground,

for the first time in years

I heard the sound

of the fresh water flowing

. . .

from deep beneath the ground.

Wounded and broken,

and a little bit slowed,

I continue my journey

listening to the flow.

Water sprites guiding

I follow

down their path

below.

∽

We are but humble servants of powers we can't even begin to comprehend

∽

AT YOUR GRAVE

I'm staring at your grave

and I'm wearing your old shoes.

I'm staring at your grave

and I'm wearing your old shoes.

Worn, and broken, battered,

retrieved from that old bin.

All of this was yours,

there wasn't any sin.

I am yours still

as I come out 'cross your grave.

It's a bitter union junction.

It's the freedom of the slave.

I'm broken, and I'm tattered, I've fallen into that old bin.

Weeping from the heavens.

Emmanuel where've you been?

Emmanuel, Emmanuel, Emmanuel you've gone.

Emmanuel, Emmanuel,

Emmanuel, where you were seen.

Emmanuel it was your home but only for a time.

The ebony and ivory,

Nor was that a crime.

It's raining from the heavens as I pass by your old church.

It's raining from the heavens and I remember that old song.

I know you'll recognise her.

How does she bear it up?

I'm standing in your shoes

and I'm standing at your side.

Tidalik is laughing

'aint done that for so long.

So many times along this path, but never for this task.

I'm travelling to your grave site

even as I drive your car.

I'm standing in your shoes now,

and I am driving in your car.

All the kings horses and all the kings men could not put us back together again.

He's having eggs for breakfast,

and we are the menu.

You can be the entrée, I'll be following soon.

Heavens flood is not enough,

you didn't want to come here too.

All I can do is drive your car along this road anew.

I've had to push myself today,

couldn't ever do it before,

with temperatures so hot as that

I had to wait for more.

I'm standing in the rain now.

I'm standing in your shoes.

No way that I can fill 'em,

now I understand the blues.

John Lee, not mistaken

knew as much as you.

How on earth did we get here?

God I'm missing you.

Eyesight overtaken!

Eyesight overtaken!

God, I've got the blues.

And he is whisking omelette

just like you used to do.

It isn't any sacrilege.

It is our, "Oh Marg," to you.

That wasn't the joke I meant.

It's our homage to you.

But the joke is well received.

It's always been the way of you.

I'm looking at your shoes now.

Can't fit them like you do.

We are driving past McDonald's.

Do you remember too?

The shame came down one birthday.

I didn't know what to do.

We all have found our limits.

It makes us human too.

I know that you are freed now.

A freeman like the slave.

I'm leading the procession, way up to your grave.

I'm cold,

and oh so lonely.

With you it never was the case.

I'm broken and I'm shattered.

You should see my face.

Should I do this solo?

No, I'm not that brave.

I've planned to do it with him.

To visit at your grave.

The rain it keeps on falling,

as it always has,

but now you're a part of it,

and I am what they have.

I'm looking at your shoes now

before I put them on.

Blurry recognition,

what I am becoming.

And I can hardly bear it,

although you know I can.

I've come to ask your blessing,

something I already have.

I'm standing at your grave now

in this pouring rain.

It's not about the feelings,

it's about the man that you became.

Standing in the sunlight

with the family,

we said goodbye, or au revoir,

though it's not the same.

He taught me poetry,

he taught me how to write,

but in these shoes,

all wet right now,

I'm looking for a knife.

Because that's the only tool

that will do the job aright.

Searching through the blur,

stumbling in the night,

we sat in that old room.

It wasn't what it was.

Now I've gone and done it,

I've poured out what I could.

My blood upon your ground here,

sacrifices made.

You are now my Isaac.

Abraham is slayed.

I'm looking at your shoes now

as I put them on.

They're battered, and we're shattered,

and he hasn't come.

Monet's all I can think of.

A gift I found for you.

Just like our final visit

to our very own Louvre.

And that's where I took the photo.

It's where you took me too.

Treasures buried centuries,

revealed once with you.

And I'm waiting at your grave

beneath the pouring rain.

We're all waiting for someone.

Someone who never came.

I'm standing in your shoes.

I'm standing at your grave.

And we are smashed and broken.

But somehow we are okay.

The slave has found his freedom.

He has run away.

I caught a glimpse at Bondi

on that special day.

And though we're not together

in that original way,

we are still together

in the original way.

Waiting at your grave site,

wearing your old shoes.

He taught me poetry,

and now I've got the blues.

VISITS

I went to my Father's grave site,

but you know he wasn't there.

I went to my Father's graveside,

but you know he wasn't there.

I went to visit you where I thought you lay,

but you had gone and left that place,

nothing left to say,

You came upon Avanti

on another day.

We are grateful for your visit.

Won't you come again?

HAD YOU

I thought that I was ready
    And now I know I'm not
    They're calling from the bleachers
    & I am going on

Oh my God
    I tried so hard
    I tried so hard for you
    I'm sorry wasn't good enough
    I'm sorry were too few

We fought & tried
    And fell apart
    We fell apart a lot
    It had us on the run now
    It had us from the start

        . . .

And though we may be gone now
    And though we may be through
    Theres a feeling that's uncanny
    That's got a lot to do with you

They're calling from the bleachers
    I love you
    In this crowd
    I thought that I was ready
    Haven't got a lot

I hear them calling out your name
    I hear that sound a lot
    You reborn
    This body
    True

We gave in not a jot
    And though you're in that other world
    And I am here not you
    I feel you all around me
    And I'm grateful
    I had you

AND I REALLY FEEL YOU'RE GONE NOW

And I really feel you're gone now
Gone for oh so long

And I really feel your absence
And it's not a pleasant song

There are no words to say it
It's the measure that you're gone

We used to drive along here
You even spoke of moving on

But we never did believe it
We just played another song

Smell the flowers
Talked for hours

Didn't seem that wrong

You always were the driver
You didn't like to ride

Our chief and our commander
No one matched your stride

But you took that big bird out of here
Upon the steep ascent

You didn't leave us willingly
You fought till you were spent

And now we live in memory
Not forgotten not alone

We see you all around the place
We hold you close to home

WATCHING SEINFELD

We always loved the joke,

"Titleist?"

We would sit there in front of the TV, Dad in his large recliner, and me perched on the three seater.

We had a good laugh.

And then we would change channels over to the footy.

That's what we did.

. . .

I say we did that because, even though I have a lump in my throat, my not saying it doesn't change the fact that he has died.

And I only sat there in front of the TV to be there with him.

The joke was only funny when we watched it together.

The footy was only good when we watched it together.

I don't watch the TV now, nor do I sit there.

I leave his chair empty, and I get out of the house, and speak these words out.

I'm walking my own dog.
    She demands a lot.

Dad's dog's name was Lucy.
    My dog's name is grief.

SEARCHING FOR A COMPASS

I'm not melancholy.
I'm just feeling into this.

This you not being around,
it's not a thing I've ever known.

And now it's the only thing I know.

And it is territory uncharted.

I'm searching for a compass.
I'm sure there's one around.

Searching for a compass,
amongst the unfound.

I'm searching for a compass
that once included you.

Searching for a compass.

One that'll be just as true.

I'm searching for a compass.

Underneath all that,
I'm searching for my father
who held me just like that.

SUMMER...GONE

Summer's over.
You have gone.

I'm flying out,
Leaving our home.

Early mornings
Too much for me.

Waiting, hopeless
Eternity.

Car is running,
Shivering cold.

Now it's real,
You've really gone.

TELL ME WHY

We had some good times here together. Though we didn't think we would.

I'm sad and I'm forlonging. You and I we could.

And now I'm coming to you,
I am coming home.

So tell me why I'm so lonely,
Tell me why I'm losing home.

LISTENING

Listening to Perfect,

And the tears come

As from the first.

Naught can be said;

It happened,

It was sad.

Still is

. . .

Perfect.

JERVIS BAY RECEDING

Jervis bay receding.
The river to the south.

Golden, slender
Lover.

Bursting at your mouth.

Staring at the sun,
to behold you
in full majesty.

Too much for anyone,
she's fleeting
on the shoreline;

waving,
waving,
waving.

On, and on,

Jervis bay receding.

My child,
Ready, gone.

Jervis bay receding.
Slender, golden brown.

Jervis bay receding.

Slow
candle
burning out.

Jervis bay receding.
The slender, and the brave.

Jervis bay receding.
If only for one day.

Jervis Bay
receding.

No more
do we go out.

A shifting,
fading shadow.
Figure with a hound.

MY NEW BOOT

My new boot is broken.
Just like that it blew.

And if I'm not mistaken.
It's a little bit like you.

Mobi-metronomey,
Leonard travelates.

Slowly going home,
and I am missing you.

Ask the strong man what to do,
'cause I haven't got a clue.

The strong man knows just what to do.

Clamp it up, and

weight it down,

then skip right out of town.

Upon the wing,
and on the road.

Doesn't matter how.

Strong man's knowing brings me heart.
So I prepare to start.

Strong man makes the way.

Folded up,
pressed right in.

Leave and go for days.

Just like him,
the Greyhound way.

Singing on the wind.

The fields lying fallow.
The strong man's making hay.

A stop,
a start,
a heart attack.

Waving me away.

I didn't know, forgive me sir,
your best
intended man.

He gave me love,
and all I did was spit upon his hand.

Another solo traveller upon this hardened ground.

We could go together, laughing with the crowd.

I didn't know,
I hadn't seen.

Forgive me now I pray.
For I have been a stranger
upon your right of way.

I thought I'd seen aright,
I thought I'd seen the way,

tearing at your Homeland
and your sovereigntay.

YOU HAVE TO GO WITH SOMETHING

You have to go with something more.

You have to go with that there is something more.

You have to go with that there is that something more,
that is that something more,
that is that something in you,
and in her.

You have to go with that something more.

That something, is this something more that is
calling you now even as you asked the question.

That something more is you.

And that something more is her.

So go with that.

Go with that something,

and go with that something more,
because that is the something more that is the
　　something that is

the sum of you

and of her.

THIS ONE DARK NIGHT

All around the scents become me.

Maraya

intoxicating me.

White in this night.

Sounds of creatures
   in the gloaming.

And I am a creature of this night.

Breeze wafting leaves.

*Gardenia scents
where the branches browned and died out.*

*Beyond the light,
    and into the night.*

*Dark night love.
    Caressing my every limb.*

*Oh yeah,
    this,
    this night.*

*This one dark night
    of love,
    of warmth,
    of breezes coming.*

*Bringing me home
    to where you sat
    with Lucy
    in the light of the Sun.*

ENDEAVOURING

We all go through different times in our lives.
    And that was a time that had to be gone through.

And now you are experiencing this time.

I have many changes happening.

Nicola will be driving herself by the end of September.

And obviously with Dad having passed my life has changed.

There is my art.
    And I'm grateful for this.

. . .

I do worry a bit about not having a formal source of income,
 but I also understand that we are part of something we don't understand.

So I'm endeavouring to relax and go with it,
 and to dance with the feelings of loss,
 and pain
 and longing,
 and allow these emotions to drive my artistic flow.

GIVING OVER

Giving over to mythology

Giving over to the truth

Giving over to the larger

Giving over to The Self

WHAT DO YOU DO?

*I'm looking out over the horizon,
waiting for the executioner to come.*

*But what if the executioner never comes?
What if nobody comes?
What then?*

Freedom?

*What do you do with your freedom?
What do you do with your time?
What do you do when you are alone?*

What do you do when you are alone with yourself?

What do you do when you are here?

What do you do if the executioner never comes?

Are you the executioner?

Or

are you your own begotten Saviour?

HORNS OF THE MOON

You are like a bull at a gate - always advancing.

Meander, and turn back on yourself.

Hers is monthly/moon calendar.

You are seeking a salve to your pain.

Learn to live with pain, with longing, with loss.

Be.

Learn to Be.

. . .

Love.

Gently move beyond anticipation.

HOW FOOLISH ARE WE?

One day we will be dead.

And then we will be a lot further apart than we are now.

So let us live while we can now before it is too late.

We have already lost ones that we love.

Are we so foolish that we would deny ourselves moments of beauty now while we can?

How foolish are we?

Hopefully not too foolish.

HIS ROSES

I have cut every single one of his roses
And placed them in a water jar.

Holding them close to my heart
I carry them to she who loved him.

The scent of the roses is the scent of him,

And it mixes with my sweat.
As I bend my back beneath the summer sun;

Each cut a memory,
Each rose a gift.

The gardener is gone.
The garden remains.

And I cut every single one of his roses
To bring to she who loved him.

*There is nothing else on this earth that I could give
to her.*

*And tonight we will remember him,
Just as we had dined with him.*

*The scent of these roses
Mixes with my sweat,
And I'm okay with that.*

WAS THERE A TIME BEFORE THIS?

Was there a time before this?
    I can hardly remember the time before your diagnosis.
    And the actual time of the disease goes back even longer.

And so you struggled.
    And we struggled,

for longer than we feel we can remember,
    now wishing there was something we could have done.

But what?

I don't know,
    though this provides no comfort as the pain of the experience remains.

REVEILLE IN 3 PARTS

PART I

*And at the end of the summer
there is water where there was none.*

*Much more water is coming
as the rains bear down upon us.*

*But much has been lost
and we remember the countless dead,*

*even as we gaze into this black pool,
unburning reflection of our world.*

Dark heart pool.

*Remembering
where we lay down,
begin again.*

PART II

Weeping at this pool of reflection.
Incapable of speech.

I sweat this out.

I wish he were in his shoes.
Or at least I in his.

Or is this just a pool of vanity?

I did not speak his name,
let us just say Daffodil.

Gazing I see myself,
not entirely happy.

Hard rock grieving.

Even this pool cannot bear me up.

A trillion singing birds,
delighting,
bringing life
again, and again
to this cold stone.

Parsifal lying by the brook.
Heart stung lover
spying
the bridge that must be crossed.

Oh so dangerous.

And thrilling too.

*Each move
threatening doom.*

*Rising up.
Drawn to you.*

*Inevitable.
Together soon.*

*Laying down
intense light dawns
upon this broken rock.*

*These angels sing
their holy round
gathered in their wings.*

*The Honey Eater's flutter dance.
Aglow
Here with her mate.*

*Subtle song,
so gentle
brings,
the lover to her home.*

PART III

*This light of love so strong that it even penetrates the
 greatest darkness.*

I would not believe it had I not beheld it.

It has something to do with the peculiarities of the light.

The light has its own intelligence, and it brings it to me.

Gathering this light within I am transformed.

MARVELLING

She said,
"Trust life",
at the spring of eternal water
upon return from my journey.

Nourishing me
with those birthday gifts
she said,
"Trust life",
diving beneath the water.

Marvelling
I followed
and she ministered to me.

Upon return from my journey
revealing her beauty, and her art,
a gift from the Indian sage.

She said,

"Trust life".

We walked upon the skillion,
among the stars
she said,
"Trust life."

At the spring of eternal water;
her song,
her music,
her art,
nourishing me upon return from my journey

PERPÉTUELLEMENT VERDOYANT

There is a strip of grass
Beneath the wall that has stayed green all summer
All the other grass is dead
Yet this strip has remained verdant
I do not understand it
Yet I love it all the same

THE SACRED WORD

Be grateful for the gifts
Each word sacred
Do not abuse the gift
Or Her
Or Them

FROM A TIME WHEN YOU BOUNCED ME ON YOUR KNEE

Laid flat
    Upon this path

Looking up
    I see your Star

Brighter than you've ever been
    Reaching out to me again

The way you held me up
    So close

Loving eyes
    Dance-ing

I know your love
    From this one pic

LANDING

Landing this way
Last time
Mid Dec
Alone
Taking pics on Nikon he was still alive

WEST, AND FURTHER WEST

Dark
Step into the night wind

The rain
The pain
Doing what I must

Orion
With whom this journey began

West
And further west

Falling off the end of the earth

Where I melt
Into
You

DESIRING THAT

>If summer were to go

>And winter also

>Then I would be happy

>Without

>Desiring

>That which

>Neither summer

>Nor the winter bring

DEEP BEYOND

The snake lays
beneath the clover.

Deep,
deep, beyond
any human calling.

As I stumble,
crying out
your name.

Penitent
to your saint,
longing for surrender.

Trudging
bootless calls.

Train never came,
cars too far.

Desertion is my name.

*But I tried
to join her.*

Threw in all I had.

*While she
was
marching westward
I had other plans.*

*Up all night,
I missed the plan,
took in half the dark.*

*Saw the crow,
and turned around,
and sat upon the grass.*

*And as we cried
we heard the sounds
of people passing by.*

*Morning came,
and went again.*

*A stranger light
then came.*

*Closing doors,
shut up the shop,*

the carriage took us out,

far beyond the fields,
away from any house.

Shots rang out,
the only sound
wings flapping
'gainst the air.

The scent of dendrite powder
settling on my hair.

EVERY MAN MUST WALK

Every man must walk alone
    But

We can
    Hold hands

And carry
    On

4:30AM

4:30am
And I am
Unsleeping

The glow of the neighbouring farmhouse
Familiar
Warm

Out here
Wind
Buffets
My father's coat

The forest echoes
Crashing
Crashing
Down

Ancient forests
Crashing

To the ground

As frogs
Oblivious
Croak on

And the neighbouring farmhouse lights
Linger

BLESSED

> We who in her
> See our eyes
>
> Bless'd by Mary
> Sanctified

After

When he was dying there was still dying left to be done

Now that he's died there's nothing

WHEN THE TASK HAS BEEN COMPLETED

*I had something to do
even though it wasn't pleasant,
or my choice.*

*It was
that thing to do,
and,
in the doing,
satisfying
pleasure
to be found.*

*Now,
my one desire
hampered
at the knees.*

*Awash with
grieving feelings,
not knowing who to be.*

*My case gone cold,
I'm stepping back
to who
is calling me.*

*A silent
call
I've heard before
in quiet
subtlety.*

WARMING SUN UPON MY FACE

Warming sun
Upon my face
As he loved so much

Lying
Dying
In his chair
Upon the Gracewood hutch

Sick bird
Nestled
Swaddled in
A child in her cot

We gave him all
We offered him
Gave him
All we've got

MY FATHER'S PASSING

My Father's passing
Becoming a not normal
Normal part of this life now

An unreal reality
A strange felt loss
An end that has happened
A loss that remains

Hollowed cavern
Like coming upon a nest
Fallen to the ground

That is what I feel
That is what I see

Thank you for walking
This with me

SEE YOU ON THE OTHER SIDE

I'm cleaning up

Their house
Their home
Their dream
Their lives

It's a messy business

Beginning and ending in darkness

Piercing pain
Memories, forgotten

You see the view
And
I feel much of the pain

Days wasted
Time

Gone

*I'll see you
On the other side*

WHEN I LEAVE

*When I leave
all of your roses are bare*

*The light is coming in fast now beneath your
    luminescent man in the moon*

But soon the man will be gone

May as well be to the other side of the world

Venus chases

Or is it the other way around?

I think it's both

*And my stomach is a leaden balloon as I wait for the
    codeine and tryptophan to kick in*

For we will party

*Again and again
And again and again and again*

Even as our shadows flicker

Possibly never to return
To this place

And yet,
Like the bush turkeys
We are still here

3 SISTERS

3 Sisters
Shrouded
Speak
Of dreaming
Time
Long
Going
On
And
Standing
Even as we rush
Home
They speak
Reminding me
They speak
We are here
We are still
Here
We remain
Here

HERE AT THE HOUSE AT VINCENTIA

Here at the house at Vincentia
I can't quite touch this
Too close
So too far
Too much
And too many
Distracting
People
And so
I'm ghost walking
Not quite present
Not quite absent
On the lookout
And wary of Jan
The memories
Faded into a melange
I'm lost
Unable to
Go there
We do our things in a mad hurry

From one to the next
And this works well for me
Saves me from
The truth
Saves me from the pain
That's way too close
That I can't handle
Not today

WEEPING

On the Scribbly gum track
We weep
Together
As we discover
On this path
Together
Our lives
Sharing
Loss
And true mourning
The violet daffodil
Silently sings
A comfort
To our weeping

HER GRACE, SHE'S BRINGING

Climbing up my father's hill
I ask of her
And she replies
A little girl
A little girl
Is coming
Coming
She
Will live
This epoch through
Guided
Guiding
Gilded
Cup
Of waters sparkling
This
Divine
Coming now
Atop this hill

Her grace
She's bringing
A whole new world

LIVING LIGHT OF YOU

This is not what I saw
This is not the
EXPERIENCE!
Oh! If you could have been
Could have seen
THIS!
Magic so strong
It put me on the ground
Never before seen
As through these black trees
The whole of the light of life is seen
Startling
Like nothing else
She winks at me
This butterfly
As we
Enjoy
This spectacle
Which I wish you could have seen
A thousand radiant candles

Rising
Enfolding me
I think that's where you like to live
In fact I know it's true
A thousand radiant candles
Screened
A living light
Of you

ROCK

Slick wet rock
speaks to me
of Peter.

Stolid,
solid,
rock.

And
the rock remains,
but we
humans
being,
we go.

Leaving
each other,
we go
somewhere else.

Our marks fade,
as the creek carries us
further away
on that first
open sweep,
unaware
of our return.

LIGHT REVEALING

*I am stripping down,
I'm going bare,
can't hide myself
anymore.*

*Out here
I stand,
I cry.*

*I'm taking flight.
Giving
all I've got tonight.*

*Flint and stone,
let the sparks fly.*

*Ignite!
Ignite!*

Ignite the night sky!

BEAUTY'S GIFT

High summer
    Peacock feathers

Beauty's gift
    Fall

Lying
    At my feet

I bow
    Collecting each

Treasure
    Bunched against my heart

. . .

My heart's
*   Glistening peacock feathers*

Spread
*   Before you*

Delicate
*   Wonders*

At your feet

Beauty's gift
*   Revealed*

RECEIVING THE BLESSING

*And at that moment
when,
resolve failing,
reaching out
you dance your love,
and offer a gesture
orchestrating the heavens
with your love.*

*Clouds,
sacred moonlight
brightening to blinding.*

*In this beauty
you
gift to me
your blessing;
pure
strength,*

*heart
to
proceed.*

WHEN OLD SHELLS BREAK

*Your suffering
Ended.
Finished,
Done.*

Now a new beginning.

*Do not weep for what you lost,
I continue being.*

*Form transformed
In beauty.*

*Living now
Anew.*

*When old shells break
We leave them,
To take another place.*

So mourn our once togetherness,
Be sad for our lost belonging.

And,
Walk on through,
In beauty,
In the light
Of new sun's rays.

AND THEN I SAW

And then I saw those same curling mists
   I hadn't seen
     Since her birth.

Silver Sun's glare
   Above
     So below.

Movement in the depths,
   Stirring of my soul.

Bringing forth
   Into the World,

My newborn,
   A girl.

AFTER THE STORM HAS PASSED

Relieved
At the passing of the storm
I breathe.

Knowing more
Than I did
When I did grieve
Upon the shore
Of my forgetting.

And
An
Unbecoming hymn,
Taken
By the moonlight.

Thoughts
Of
Coming in.

MUSHROOM FLOWERS

Mushroom
Flowers
Here
Now
Life
Brings
Decay
If not from ashes
The least
Remains
Rise again
Skyward

TWO DUCKS

Two ducks swim
Side by side.

Silently
They swim

Across
Still water.

RETURNING TO THIS OLD GIANT
(TOGETHER AGAIN)

I rest upon her.

Soothing gentle rain
Upon my face.

And
I know
Ultimately
We won

A victory of sorts.

Not over that which cannot be defeated.

But,
Rather,
Ourselves,

As we sat there
Together,

As I do now,

With you here,

Soft, cooling rain upon my face.

And I realise,
This giant's falling,
Not an accident.
But an inevitability

Of life,
Presenting
A challenge
For us
To find

New growth
Together.

POSTSCRIPTUM

*I once nursed a sick man
Who was dying for a year.*

*An initiation
For both of us.*

*His speech staccato,
Mine sadly inadequate.*

*But the books they helped.
I read to him*

In amongst the tears.

*Some days I was over it,
Others barely coped.*

*I once nursed a sick man
Who was dying for a year.*

*We didn't know each week
If that would be his last.*

*We simply helped support him,
Helping with each task.*

*Incapable,
Slowing down,*

The wounded bull laid down,

*Unpleasant groanings
Were his only sound.*

*It came upon us quickly.
We were unprepared.*

*Unpeaceful in the quiet,
The suffering shouted out.*

*We no longer travelled,
Were lucky to go out.*

*Eventually he closed his eyes
Didn't make a sound.*

*The door was closed,
Lights turned out,*

And so I write this now.

NOTES

For Auld Lang Syne, My Dear

1. The Title of the poem "For Auld Lang Syne, My Dear" references the New Year's Eve poem of remembrance by the Scottish poet, Robert Burns. And the last lines are my own incorrect note from memory referencing the final lines of William Stafford's "The Way It Is" which my daughter read to Dad in the week before he passed.

INSIDE OUT HEART

Volume 2: Diary notes of being with my dying father

SJP Dooley

Dedicated to the carers at the Sydney Adventist Hospital, Mt Wilga Rehab Hospital and The Gracewood Aged Care Centre

Go down to your deep old heart, and lose sight of yourself.
And lose sight of me, the me whom you turbulently loved.

— D.H. LAWRENCE (FROM KNOW THYSELF, KNOW THYSELF MORE DEEPLY)

PREFACE TO VOLUME 2: DIARY NOTES OF BEING WITH MY DYING FATHER

These are the diary notes I made as I was caring for Dad during his dying year. At each moment we did not know that this final period of time would, in fact, last as long as a year. We thought he was gone in January, and in each subsequent month we thought it would likely be his last, or second last month. He lived on, however, so that like the boy who cried wolf, his eventual passing took us by surprise. Not because it wasn't inevitable, but, rather, because the inevitable had sat on the event horizon for so long we'd all found ourselves locked into a routine, the nature of which is recorded herein. I've endeavoured to bring the immediacy of each moment to you, and to invite you in to our times in the hospital, the rehab centre and the nursing home. This has been a confronting task, both in the doing, and in the collating of this volume. This second volume carries an unvarnished truth, difficult to bear, however, necessary as a conveyor of solidarity to those who find themselves in this position. Most of the writing in these pages comes from messages I would write to myself in each moment. Looking back on them now I've noticed a prayer-like quality to them. There is a comfort I received from the meditative nature of writing these notes to myself during these times of aloneness, incapacity and seeping loss.

My hope is for you, as you make your way down this road, that this collection will feed your soul, and provide you with the comfort that comes from recognition, and knowing others have, likewise, travailed a similar struggle.

SJP Dooley 2020

SUNDAY 3 FEBRUARY

Pa saying to Nicola,

"I wish I could just get up and do things. I wish we didn't have to sleep. I wish we could just get up and do things you know. I want to be able to do things. I don't want to be stuck here unable to do anything."

TUESDAY 12 FEBRUARY: INTO THE KINGDOM OF BEAUTY

Walking alone as my father undergoes his operation I am gingerly making my way down through the crooked, and winding creek. It is a trackless place where I must find my way anew with each careful step. I am alone, it is getting dark, the mosquitoes are coming out, and I do not really know where I am, or what to do. A sign from the local water authority says to stay away, a sure signal that this is the place to be. It really is getting dark, and I really do not know where to go as I crash my way down the steep rocky incline, trying not to get myself injured, and trying not to get completely lost in the darkness.

I nearly tripped on sticks, and tangling vines, and I keep on walking, slightly confused as to where I am, but feeling that this is the way to go, when in my peripheral vision I make out your appearance. You're all dressed in blue, shimmering, and have shining light and goodness. You rest for a moment to allow our encounter to begin and then you engage me in circles. In circles upon circles. An ancient dance ritual of greeting. You welcome me, this clumsy stranger who has been away from this place for longer than memory, this incredulous traveller, this sojourner in the form of a man, and across so many different places and spaces you know me and you welcome me with the coming of the dusk. You welcome me to your home, to your sanctuary. You also have travelled much and changed significantly, in fact, you are not what you once were, for you were once a caterpillar, eating, crawling, and then you...

...you were always becoming this beautiful blue butterfly that you are now, and you knew it, and your own sisters knew it, and your cells knew it, and your imaginal cells knew it, and now you are that which you were always becoming. If only we could see what each of us is becoming then maybe we would be a little bit easier on ourselves, and each other. You always knew that you had to be who you were at each stage of your existence. You were a caterpillar but you also had the imaginal cells of the beautiful, blue butterfly within you. You could not immediately be the butterfly. You had to be the other. It's what you were always becoming so it was simply best to not kill the grub, but to allow the path to keep on doing its thing, and for you to keep on eating. It wasn't easy as you continued to grow on your inevitable path towards butterfly-hood but you were always going to be a butterfly despite what anybody said or did, and no matter how disgusted others were by your grubby-ness. You were always going to become a butterfly and this is how old became pretty. New. This is a truth that nobody and nothing could deny or take away. You just kept on eating, and eating, and eating as you were the very hungry caterpillar. And just like the very hungry caterpillar you have become your true butterfly. You show me that no matter what happens, Dad is becoming, he's becoming, in and through his imaginal cells, and I thank you dear butterfly for your goodness and sharing of yourself to me on this most auspicious evening.

I think of you now in your butterfly hollow, sitting there so tranquilly and so beautifully as I hear the distant traffic sounding past and you, continuing to simply be, beautiful being that you are, and were, and always have been regardless of what others might have said, or thought about you during your time embodied as a grub. And I thank you for simply being. Thank you for gracing me with your presence on this most telling day. Thank you for visiting on this day, for being a butterfly on the eve of Valentine's Day, for you came to me in your beauty, in your silence, your wings held together in your own silent prayer, beauty of love, of wonder.

A sign of transformation, and that all is well. I thank you dear butterfly of love, for that is what you are as you hold your space within.

Thank you.

WEDNESDAY 13 MARCH: FINDING MY CAR WINDOW SMASHED & EVERYTHING STOLEN

Think about how you feel about what you've lost, and then think, REALLY THINK about what Dad is losing.

Immeasurably more.

Sit with that man.

And be with that.

Really contemplate that Dad is losing everything material.

And just hold his hand as you would like to be comforted now, and told everything's going to be alright.

And let him know everything's going to be alright.

Absorb this lesson and how you feel now, and how agitated and activated you are, and how much you need comfort, and how others provide that to you, and how you can provide that to Dad.

DEAR DAD

Dear Dad,

Ultimately I have to let you go.

You were running your race in this life long before I was running my race.

I simply need to have compassion.

Parents normally die before their children.

That is the natural order of things.

You are a big, heavy man and it is too much for me to prop you up indefinitely.

You are doing your best.
I have done my best, the brothers are doing their best, Mum is doing her best, Bob is doing his best, Nicola is doing her best, as is everyone.

DAD CAN'T WALK

Dad can't walk.

He is bedridden.

It is not that he does not want to walk, it is that he cannot walk.

Let this truly sink in.

He loved to play golf and he can no longer do that.

The chances of Dad being able to play golf again are virtually non-existent.

In fact, even in me saying that I am most likely gilding the lily.

Gilding the lily, as he is unlikely to really be able to do much.

I should see if I can talk privately with Alan Lam about this today.

I must remember to only talk about Dad's condition and issues privately without him, or others around.

I am returning to my initial comments:

Dad can't walk;

Even Mum can walk.

Dad has always been a very active person and his inability to walk must be such a terrible thing for him.

Dad can't walk.

He is completely reliant on others for everything:

- Toileting

- Showering

- Getting in and out of bed

- Being fed

- Drinking.

Even any forms of entertainment such as TV, or obtaining books.

He cannot even reach around to answer the telephone.

When I am away from him it is very difficult for me to be able to communicate with him, so I do videos from him to people.

Unfortunately, I'm the only person that does videos of him to people.

I know how much I would appreciate seeing the videos so I will seek to keep doing them. In fact, I will do a reminder to myself now to keep on doing the videos for Dad.

SUNDAY 2 APRIL: AT ALICE ROBINSON RESERVE

Dad and Lucy came here all the time.

And Mum lived there.

Now they are all gone and only we are left.

And yet I can still see Nicola, and Dad, and Lucy there at the swings and the seats.

But that time has gone.

And only I am left.

Nicola is with her boyfriend, Pat.

And Dad is struggling with many things including his loneliness, at Gracewood Retirement Village.

And it's all painful.

And sorrowful.

And hard work.

And such loss.

Such loss.

Dad, who so easily walked up to this small park, will no longer be walking up here again.

And it's so sad and upsetting.

And I really don't know what to do.

Because there isn't anything I can do.

It is all past.

So I stop and I smell the white rose at Jim the Roseman's place, the one that gives me the feeling of drinking fresh lemonade.

∼

A monarch butterfly came and just lightly touched my heart and flittered away

∼

To the people Dad has a great sense of humour and the absurd, but in our lives he was the straight man to our antics, often bewildered, most times amused, always proud.

AND HE HAD MANY STORIES

On our last visit to The San Hospital, as he was receiving his Avastin infusion he told the nurse of his client who had been charged with stealing the Sunday Newspaper, the Police alleging his client picked up the paper & skipped down the street singing "Sunday just isn't Sunday without the Sunday Telegraph."

He'd tuck us into bed, and say a prayer for us.

He had a John Denver cassette tape, and we'd play "Grandma's feather bed" over and over again on our way to pick up fresh hot bread on Sunday morning from the Stone Bakery in Emu Plains in his green BMW 3.0S.

He loved cricket, and the Manly Sea Eagles.

He was a fast bowler with a windmill action, and we simply called him "Destructor" because he was so good. He was a competitive sportsman and played to win. Our family played Spotto on our car trips, and Dad, being in the driver's seat had the best view and used it to full advantage cutting no shrift, "Spotto" would ring out from the driver's seat and we would just have to cop it. He loved puns, wordplay, and jokes, and could remember them perfectly.

He helped me immensely. He always supported me. And he helped me to become who I am today. I am grateful to have had him for as long as I did, and he lives on in all of us.

Thank you.

Dad has left an impression on all of us. His golfing partner, Mike, hasn't had a good round of golf since Dad's diagnosis. So, immediately upon being released from prison, I mean hospital, we went to Twin Creeks. Dad leapt into a golf buggy, and said, "they're out on the back 9."

I said, "But didn't Professor Owler say not to drive a car?"

"A car," he shouted above the wind, "A car. This is a golf buggy on a private range, and not subject to the Motor Traffic Act."

Approaching a rise at full speed Mike was waving his hands in what we thought was a greeting, but, was, in fact screams of, "No, no, no. Stop, Peter, Stop!" I screamed like Homer Simpson, as belatedly Dad slammed on the brakes, the buggy hovering at the tip of the edge of the largest sand bunker on the course.

"It shouldn't have done that," said Dad, "they've got GPS limiters to keep you on the track."

"Not that one," shouted Mike. "Look at the clubs on the back. You've stolen a Member's private buggy and they don't have the limiters."

Turning to me Dad said, "I don't think Professor Owler needs to know about this Sime."

∼

THERE'S A MOMENT in my ayahuasca journeying where we are in a timeless moment & Dad & I are sparkling, shining stars in the sky of the universe, in space.

∼

AT DEX RANDALL'S THURSDAY MORNING MEN'S STRESS GROUP

Sydney Royal Botanic Gardens

"Be specific about the stress.
Don't generalise.
Address the specific facts."

And I reach into my pocket and there's a golden key there.

Thank you Dex.

I hear Elvis' *"We're caught in a trap.
I can't get out..."*

And I'm back at that rose garden where I first brought one of my first loves. And there's that same familiar scent, intoxicating, powerful, heady, an undeniability to it.

A woman with a monk's shaved head walks by.

Dex taught – "bring it back to the specific."

You have to get in real close to taste the scent of the rose.

In your situation with feeding Dad at lunch, be ok with the mess. Think of how much you are helping Dad in his helpless state, and the understaffed, overworked carers who all benefit greatly from your being there.

And the gardener slowly works away at his slow and meticulous task.

IN HIS FINAL DAYS

You are with your Father in his final days. You need to come to terms with this.

He refuses to do all of the things that could help him.

This is very hard.

And also wondering whether, even if he was to engage in all the self-care, whether it would be enough anyway.

I've also come to realise that others don't understand, and that this poses its own challenges.

I have to accept.

Accept and adapt.

Accept that it is what it is.

You have to let it go, and you have to let him go.

We are all choosing all the time.

Sure, it's based on our situation and circumstances, but nevertheless each of us is making the choices that we are making.

And all of these visitors keep pumping Dad with junk food because they figure that he's a dying man and should have these treats for some kind of quality of life, rather than realising that if he was given all healthy stuff then he could well not be a dying man.

The tragicomedy of life.

ALLOW DAD HIS SOUL HEALING

Allow Dad his soul healing.

Allow Dad his soul healing.

Allow Peter Dooley his soul healing.

Only he can undertake that particular path.

Listen to him.

Listen.

Be present and actively listen.

Be a healing presence.

Read and re-read the book about being a healing presence.

The healing presence.

Just listen and be there and allow him to win his arguments.

There is nothing left to do now but to be there with him.

Just be there with him and listen to him.

Read to him from the Guru of Golf.

HIS EXPERIENCE

∼

There has been shame, and embarrassment, and frustration, and loss of pride for Dad in his experience with his incapacity.

∼

Dad:

"*I thought I was dying this morning and I was very, very grateful*

I want to die

I want to die

I want to die

I want to die

I want to die

I want to die

I want to die

I'm just thinking of my dear Mother

She just went to sleep one night and they rang us in the morning and said she died during the night."

∼

SO FAR APART

There are small preschool children running around in constant action and chatter, scrambling, and leaping, hair flying behind, trailing as they leap.

They are in Gracelands Daycare Early Education Centre.

They are across the road but millenia apart from here.

We are in The Gracewood Retirement Village.

The two are so far apart.

So far apart.

18 APRIL: THURSDAY BEFORE EASTER

At breakfast table alone half an hour after everyone's left.

I wheel him out and ask him to move his right leg up so I can put his right foot on the plate of his wheelchair.

He refuses:

"Why should I?"

I'm working at his feet and I notice the top of the compression stocking is digging into his calf severely.

He's still completely uncooperative and says:

"I'm quite comfortable here" and stubbornly stymies my efforts to help.

So I walk off and leave him to contemplate that for a while.

We are moving out of his room on level 1 today so I go and start packing up.

I return and there are two nurses struggling with all their might, both working on both his feet.

His feet are so swollen that they have to work with everything they've got to get his compression stockings off.

Nurse Sheila tells me she'll go and try and find some larger compression stockings.

Dad asks me:

"There's nowhere you can get them from Sime?"

I reply: "Nowhere."

Dad: "You can't get any?"

Me: "No."

Nurse Sheila goes away to search for some stockings large enough.

I offer to wheel him outside into the sun.

He accepts and I wheel him out into the sun.

I don't know what we'd do if we weren't having sunny days.

Sitting with his face in the sun is some of the only relief he gets. Because that's what it's about now. It's not about joy or satisfaction or happiness. It's just the occasional moment of brief relief.

11:15am Ashley is giving him his massage in the sun and he says it's very soothing.

One of my first memories of Dad is him holding me on a surf mat in the roiling whitewash. Holding me, and the mat ready to launch. I'd like to say, I was equally terrified and thrilled, but I wasn't.

~

When I was about 10 years old and Dad was nearing 40 he took up early morning jogging around Lapstone Oval. And having worked hard for decades without regular exercise he could only plod around the track. I, on the other hand, was full of all the vigour of emerging youth. And, with the insensitivity to match, I would tease Dad and remind him each time I lapped him. But one thing I always wondered was why he always looked so happy even though he was so slow. I've since discovered the source of his joy as I've watched my own daughter running rings around me in similar ways.

ON THE PASSING OF JOHN GOODISON (REUNION)

I have this image of a young 19 year old woman, Shirley Churm walking into the Gracewood through the sliding doors.

Fully human.

Real.

And pressing the lift button, and waiting for the lift and then going up in the lift to level one and the lift doors open up, and she walks out and down the corridor and she walks into John's room and he smiles that smile of his.

And she holds out her hand.

And the 21 year old John climbs out of the 84 year old John and they embrace.

MONDAY 29 APRIL

Weeping, inconsolable. Listening to John Denver - "Annie's Song" by Dad's bedside.

I thought of my Dad - the bright shining ship of light embarking on a voyage into a dark unknown ocean, horizon and sky.

The earliest image I have of my father and I is a black-and-white picture of a handsome, dark haired man holding a tiny nondescript bundle in the way that you hold a baby. I'm told that bundle is me.

EARLY MEMORIES

I can't say that I have an actual first memory of us together because somehow it seems that he had simply always been there.

I do have some very strong recollections of growing up with Dad as the father of Phillip, Simon and Matthew.

I had severe allergies as a child. I would get a rash called urticaria that felt like my skin was in flames. Dad took me to see the Macquarie Street allergy specialists. One early morning we stood together in front of the Manly Ferry at Circular Quay. We'd been up since before sunrise to catch the train from Lapstone down from the Blue Mountains. It was a rare opportunity for us to be in the city for breakfast and Dad, always the gourmand, with anticipation on his lips said to me, "How about Pancakes at The Rocks?"

With all of my eight-year-old boys exuberance I too was excited to be in the city for breakfast and replied:

"I would like a pie and sauce."

I can still see the disappointment as his face drained of hope for those hot buttered pancakes and we went and had a pie and sauce.

I did feel somewhat relieved recently when we were at Mount Wilga Hospital and Dad said that all he was craving was a pie and sauce. However I do regret not being old enough, and wise enough, at the time, to give him his Pancakes at The Rocks breakfast opportunity.

AND WHAT THEN?

I feel like Roy Hobbs from The Natural.

And of course he was based on Parzifal.

And just before she shot the sacred wound into him she said:

And what then?

And what then?

And what then?

I must go on my path. Not the path my Father or Mother or anyone else has for me.
I must go on my own path

SATURDAY 8 JUNE

Dad expressed today that one of his only disappointments was that he hadn't been able to make it back home.

SUNDAY 9 JUNE
(QUEENS BIRTHDAY LONG WEEKEND)

1:15pm in the sun with Phil the fireman. And his daughter Kate comes to take him to see Red Joan at the movies.

Kate asks me if I come every Sunday.

And I say every day.

She's amazed.

I'm right there with Dad so I don't say it's because he's dying.

I join Phil into the conversation and say something about how these times demand it of us or something.

And he agrees.

TUESDAY 11 JUNE

Who knows re: visitors. Dad's position on things seems to vary. She misinterpreted Dad's comment that "I don't want to talk" to be that he didn't want to see people. He's always been extroverted and has many, many relationships. Obviously people that he's never been close friends with, and who lack the subtlety he needs, like X, exert negative value on him. But there are certain people like B, R, us three boys and our family's, who he always willingly wants more of, especially the grandchildren. And then, there is the nature of the circumstance. These people are never going to see him again. And that is a significant consideration for me. Other than X, he hasn't told me of anyone that he specifically doesn't want to see. He has told me that people can come as long as he doesn't have to talk, and can sleep. Sure, people like Z, aren't "easy" but it seems that there's something there by way of a relationship that still provides a ticket in to see Pete. He absolutely loved the visit from John "Selmesy" Selmes and Robin Caffrey when Phil was here. John is an old Manly Court of Petty Sessions buddy, like John "Squizzy" Taylor.

WEDNESDAY 12 JUNE

I feel I've got carers fatigue : (

∼

THURSDAY 13 JUNE

Coming to terms with my Father's dying is not an easy thing to do for me, let alone for him, or for any of the rest of the family. It is not something that comes to you constantly in a linear fashion but something that you feel.

It pulses and you feel it.

You feel it in a whole bunch of different ways.

It is a loss that keeps on coming to you.

It is a pain in the pit of the gut.

It is a sudden onset of weakness and malaise.

It is not something wanted or called for.

It is a generally confronting and upsetting overall feeling of something more than what the word discomfort tends to connote.

It is the sadness at the loss of everything for the man.

There is a joylessness to it. A sad, upsetting helplessness, contingent upon circumstances completely outside of one's control.

I'm reading a book by Francis Weller called something like On The Wild Edge of Sorrow and the book speaks of the benefits of grief. I am embracing the book to try to find something, because I need something.

I suppose just like my Father's enjoyment of the warm sun on his face I just experience the same thing with the warm sun on my face.

At times I feel extremely wasted. For now, all I can think about strangely is a green tea.

The sun is shining and it is an incredible comfort.

It is an unseasonably warm morning and there is a warm breeze blowing.

I never know what I'm going to walk into when I see Dad.

We have a friend due to arrive at 10am today and just like those people that friend will come in full of life and surety.

It's fucking depressing.

This. The whole thing in here. Dad. The visitors. The other residents. The smells. The sounds. The experience.

Dad wants us to make sure he's dead before the lid is put on the coffin. This has been worrying him all week, to the point where he was asking for the chaplain.

"I'm sure I'm not the first one to have this concern."

I promised him that I'd ensure that he had died before the lid was put on the coffin.

He asked us to do the same for Mum.

And he wants me to bring Mum around to see him again.

MONDAY 15 JULY – DAD'S DREAM OF THE GLOWING BLUE ORB

Dad has a dream of nothingness.

A dream of people being placed into a glowing blue Orb.

He said:

"It was like that book you read me."

(Referring to Stephen Jenkinson's "Die Wise")

He said:

"I shouldn't be here. I'm taking up space."

And he said:

"There was one other thing."

I asked:

"What was that?"

He said:

"I was warm and comfortable."

I said:

"And that's a good thing."

He agreed:

"Yes, a very good thing."

CHALLENGES - Fatigue

From my experience with my father I have found that the task of caring for him day in, day out, has led to me feeling extremely emotionally and physically fatigued.

SO MUCH OF DAD'S LIFE IS OVER

So much of Dad's life is over already.

It's a very sad thing and that's very hard for me to admit but it's the truth.

We have to admit it.

We have to face the truth for what it is, and the way that our situation and our existence is.

He has lost most of his life already.

He is constrained to a bed that he cannot escape from.

He is stuck in a room that he cannot leave, and that his condition has made him to not want to leave anyway.

It is a life that has been reduced.

It has been constricted and shrunk down to a very small dot already.

I must accept this.

Everyone, including all visitors and carers need to accept this.

It is a hard, painful, difficult confronting truth to accept.

For someone who was always active and always on the go and a sportsman, being incapacitated must be so difficult for Dad.

SUNDAY 4 AUGUST

Feeling overwhelmed about whole situation with Dad.

And all the uncertainty.
  And not knowing.

And everything...

SUNDAY 11 AUGUST

The subjects for today, sex, and death, both inevitable forces/experiences that we struggle with so much:

Death. Taking us from inhabiting the body.

Sex. Continuing our life force within a body, but different bodies. The lover's body and the offspring. And I was always taught that all of this was so shameful. And even now it is very culturally taboo stuff, relegated to places of non-reality like media, books, TV, films, publications, magazines, websites.

But these are strong, powerful forces that exist and push us. It is said that a man will go without food and water to get together with a woman. And this force, this overwhelming force is related to death. Sex has "Le petit mort" - the little death and then capital "D" Death is the concluding, the big "D" Death where the inhabitation of the body and life within that body ceases and then what?

Grief

Loss

Frustration

High emotions

Upset

A feeling of falling away:

For all involved, the dying person and the carers, family, friends, relatives, nursing/care staff, these feelings, emotions and forces are all unbidden and unintended and uncontrolled. Real, and at times of our life, like when we are a teenager/adolescent, so overwhelming, so overpowering, so strong, like the inevitable rising of the sun and the passing away of the sun in to night and the darkness of the night, these things are inevitable, and uncontainable, and uncontrolled, and uncontrollable. We exist within all of this. Thoroughly within it all. These things don't "happen " to us - they are us and we are them.

I dreamt I saw an old teenage friend in my dreams. She, having grown into a mother and changed significantly:

-less fun;

-less spontaneous;

-very serious.

Joseph Campbell - JC speaks of taking the right hand path or the left-hand path.

Question: What are you going to do?
And now I revel in the rising of the morning sun, just as I revel in her nakedness. The overwhelming strength and power and beauty of this emergent, emerging sun, so bright I cannot even look at it. and that is the absolute trademark of it - that it is so bright "I cannot even look at it."

Is that not just like sex and death - that ultimately it is so much. So much, that though I revel within the experience of this life, this life-giving, this beauty, ultimately the power is too much, too much for me, and though I experience it, I cannot truly face it fully without going blind, and so it must be a glance/askance that I am only ever experiencing it side on, but never fully. And I exist in this small body, touched by it, while it is all and all life-giving, the cause of life, the life force, and, I, a mere passenger that has all but to relax into this and to receive it all:

-the love;

-the light;

-the unbearable blindingness of it;

-the life of it, and I, for now, and all that comes into and out of being;

because this light is golden, and all that's golden is always good, so…go with it. Go with it, and be blessed by it, for it is all good, and if you can open yourself to seeing it all through this golden light you will see that all is, and are, manifestations of this golden orb of power just as your Father had his dream of the glowing orb with people being placed in it, and it was all peaceful, and safe, and warm, and good, and even now this proximate star proceeds to bathe me in her golden glory, and I at once overwhelmed, and captivated am held in aesthetic arrest, and comfort, and peace.

All of this provides me with feelings of peace, and comfort, and feeling love ,and support, and acceptance, and that it's okay :)

WEDNESDAY 21 AUGUST

Thickened liquids are freaky things. We struggle with it all. The straw gets left in his mouth when he pulls the cup away, and it just dangles from his mouth like a giant cigarette.

And he angles the cup as if to drink from the cup, and it goes everywhere. So in the end, although we should be really using the straw, we tossed it.

"Is Phil still around?"

"Phil's in South Africa."

"So, it's you and Matthew."

"Chuck's in San Francisco."

"I just have to let Professor Bowler know I don't intend driving."

"Tuesdays are B's yoga days."

Had good conversations.

Dad told me he didn't have any visitors today, but then Bob Peacock sent me a message saying that Bob had been here at lunchtime today. So, Dad's short term memory is quite unreliable.

He asked me to confirm both nurse call buttons many, many times.

Closing eyes a lot at end of meal.

Both eating and drinking is a messy business. Now with the thickened drinks, drinking with a long handled small spoon is quite a messy trip.

Met young male Nurse Harry with the sparkling earring and the spiky hair.

Kept asking for pillows round the back of his neck even though he had them there.

He slid over so far to the right that I asked him to press his nurse call button. And he had a lot of trouble doing that. He turned his light on first etc...

Left eye twitching out of control so we called for the RN.

It seems to be a new thing.

Stopped twitching.

THURSDAY 22 AUGUST

We wrap him up in his beanie and Sea Eagles scarf and go out into the sun. He loves having his face in the sun.

I need to write wholeheartedly

I need to write wholeheartedly and without any censoring because everybody is going to fall away from these bodies anyway.

Write with love about the inspiring individual.

Don't hold back.

Go for it.

Write whatever comes into your head.

No more pre-censoring and no more censoring.

Write of the pain and the pleasures, and what it is to be human, and what it is to exist in the ways that you have seen people existing, and trying, and doing what they can, like a cyclist trying to ride up a hill.

RS is a proponent of being positive and while I may not agree with him about the particular things to be positive about it's a very good approach to take to your life and to your thinking and to your work, so in my case that involves being positive about my creative work, even if I am writing from a place of depression, or anxiety, or sadness, or frustration, or loss, or any other area of upset, or challenge, or difficulty.

I must work on this issue within myself, and understand how this is the way

It's very lonely and some other word I can't find to express the feelings/emotions, but it's something of emptiness like a small ship in the night sitting precariously on a vast endless ocean

MONDAY 23 SEPTEMBER

12:45pm while I feed him lunch:

"One of the ladies was going to..."

"What's that?"

No reply.

Me: "You mean one of the nurses was going to feed you lunch?"

Dad: "Yes."

"Just gotta watch out for the lions and the tigers."

Who knows what that meant???

Dozing most of the time.

Looks at me and says:

"I just find it hard with X sometimes. Have you noticed that?"

"Yes."

"He has his own views as to how everything should be run."

Then dozes again.

Wakes up and has chocolate mousse and cream dessert.

Stops eating, wipes mouth and announces:

"14."

"14 what?"

"I had 14 wipes of my mouth."

Dozes.

Awakens and eats more choc mousse and dessert.

Then he wants a coffee and he enjoys it very much.

EMOTIONAL OVERLOAD

There are all these photos of Dad throughout the house, and when I look at them I can't help but be overwhelmed by sadness from the fact that in each of those photos he had no idea that it would all come to this.

And seeing those photos, and then being with him in his current state of absolute incapacity every day pushes me into a strange state of emotional overload that is overwhelming, and at the same time impossible to express.

I NEED MORE SUPPORT

I need more support with caring for Dad.

It has not been easy.

I am very grateful for the support that I'm receiving from Mike and Cin.

This is hard.

It is undeniably hard.

FRIDAY 27 SEPTEMBER

Pretty much paralysed now at the time of awakening first thing in the morning. Each morning when I come in he's in increasingly unnatural positions slumped and completely incapable of moving at all. Doesn't seem to really be able to move right side much anymore while sleeping in the night...is propped up with all kinds of pillows on left and right.

He is left by staff until everyone else's breakfast is just about finished before he gets his, and by then he's often starving.

And he's not happy about it at all.

The problem is that there are simply not enough people to do all the jobs. So if I wasn't here I don't know when he'd be attended to. It's similar to the problem of getting out in the morning sun before it gets too hot. We can't get him outside because he's trapped in his bed because we have to wait until the nurses are ready to come and wash him and transfer him. But that gets quite late in the day.

I get him his porridge and I get prunes and feed it to him with my 2 long spoon system.

Says he wants to speak to the kitchen to thank them for the delicious porridge.

Nurse Miriam arrives and pleads with him to give him a shave today and he agrees.

Then he declined getting medications.

But subsequently agrees to meds and washes it down with coffee.

We do a video to Bob.

He wanted some more porridge so I went and got two more bowls and they were dispatched hastily.

Leaning even more to the right now.

Very big "Pa stares."

Then sleeping and leaning far to the right.

It's like he's going underwater.

Red eyes.

Keeps eyes closed while nurse Kim talks to him about shaving him.

SATURDAY 5 OCTOBER

Has been awake for a while waiting for porridge.

Very keen for porridge.

Wants me to add prunes from my prune stash.

Reading the Australian prunes packet and very excited.

"I'm ready for these."

Loving his porridge and prunes.

It's like feeding a baby bird.

Mouth opens and in it goes.

Mouth opens and in it goes.

Second bowl of porridge.

Asks and receives more prunes from me from our stash.

The consumption of the porridge is a slow process with dozing during the process.

And off to sleep before finishing second bowl.

Soundly off to sleep.

Carol Stirling is coming in at lunchtime today.

Left hand very, very bad. Like a swollen lump of meat with bad bleeding and indentations. Very sore.

SUNDAY 6 OCTOBER

Walking into his darkened room I reach across to pull up the blind.

He's laying with his neck pushed back and before anything else: "Porridge would be good."

And we are on!

Before any lights are turned on, or the blinds are up - it is porridge time.

The prunes are added from the stash and we are into it. I feed him with a spoon in each hand, Edward Scissorhands style, right spoon, left spoon, right spoon, as fast as I can go to keep up. If I pause I hear, "a bit more" and serve it up followed by "Thank you."

Loving his porridge and prunes.

Didn't want to do any videos.

Eating prunes.

Chewing on them with eyes closed like a cow chewing cud.

Nurse Dipa checks on us.

Chef Terri is holding a second bowl of porridge warm for us in the kitchen.

He's really not interested in Canberra Raiders v Eastern Sydney Roosters.

Eats.

Dozes.

Old lady across the hallway screams at her husband:

"Have you had your fruit salad?"

Something unintelligible from her husband.

"I gave it to you in a jar."

"You have a spoon in your hand!"

"You're gonna have to ask for your hearing aids."

"What's that love?"

Eating - dozing - eating - dozing.

Saw Dr B for the first time in a long time yesterday.

"Got my eye fixed."

Dozing.

Fell right asleep eating second bowl but was able to eat a bit more later.

MONDAY 7 OCTOBER

Sleeping which is not surprising as Daylight Saving has just started so we are doing everything an hour earlier.

I'm quietly sitting there letting him sleep but the cleaner comes and knocks on the door and wakes him, and as he opens his eyes:

"How's the porridge?"

I go to get his porridge but Nurse Dipa is already coming with his porridge and brings it in.

Dipa asks if I'm feeding him.

We ask him and he says:

"Staff."

He's having terrible trouble finding his words.

Repeating:

"The um…"

"The um…"

And we don't know what he's talking about.

And then Dipa brings the porridge into view and he says:

"Yes. That's it."

He was trying to say that he wanted the porridge.

Smashed first bowl of porridge.

Interested to hear that the Sydney Roosters beat the Canberra Raiders in the grand final.

Gets into second bowl.

Finishes second bowl and nurse asks if he wants a coffee.

She gets him a coffee and he dozes the whole time.

This morning he was sleeping the most I've seen since January. We hardly interacted the whole time as he was sound asleep other than when he was being fed.

TUESDAY 8 OCTOBER

Loving his second bowl of porridge being fed by his nurse.

Didn't sleep well. Awake a bit. Not in pain.

After being awake through the night was very ready for his porridge.

Plenty of "Pa stare."

He was interested to hear of Nicola's "Learner driving."

The nurse obtains a large soup spoon and does something I've never seen before. She spoon feeds him his thickened coffee with the soup spoon. I don't know if this is an indication that his capacity has reduced to being less able to drink from the cup...

The lady across the hallway is telling her friend about how her husband rolled out of bed onto the floor in the night. Her friend is asking if he then slept on the floor.

Her friend says: "When he falls out of the bed he obviously doesn't get hurt."

As soon as nurse stops feeding him his eyes close and he's off to a strong sleep again. No conversation between us at all after nurse goes. Things have changed.

Didn't want to do a video.

Clocked out into a very deep sleep.

WEDNESDAY 9 OCTOBER

Cousin Jayne has told me that uncle Len is coming to visit Dad at 12 noon today for Dad's birthday.

Soundly sleeping and snoring.

Right leg involuntarily kicking up and down at the knee while sleeping.

Woke up and into porridge.

Didn't want to do a video.

Dozing through first bowl.

Seems to be dozing even more today.

Eyelids appear like they're holding some fluid and left eyelid is scarred from the problem that's been there.

I prompt him to feed him more of his porridge.

If he keeps going like this he won't be conscious for feeding and then what? I seek to discuss this with the RN and level 2 Manager, Pretty Sharma but Pretty was unavailable so I'll need to talk to her later.

I haven't seen him bring his right hand out from under the covers for several days.

I get second bowl.

I told Dad how he'll be having lots of Bday visitors and he said:

"I'll just sleep through them."

He's looking quite sad when awake and quite peaceful when dozing.

I talk to him about prunes and he says:

"Down near Wombat"

I think he might have read the Angas Park brand on the prune packet and was commenting that Angas Park is down near Wombat.

I told him how they've just discovered the log book from Noah's Ark which reads:

"Day 17: unicorns taste delicious."

He loved it.

Dozing while chewing a prune he very much resembles a cow chewing its cud.

Just kept asking for more prunes today.

Must've had at least 9.

He wanted a third bowl of porridge, but unfortunately we take so long to eat, by the time he asked for it, it was 9:50am and there was no porridge left.

So I gave him another prune.

I went searching, found a banana yogurt and presented it to him like a proud hunting cat laying a dead bird down in front of its master.

"No."

"You don't want it?"

"There's no porridge left so this is all I could find."

"No."

"Well as you'd say 'that's a matter entirely for you.'"

"It is…[pause]…I think I'll have another nap."

Closes eyes and chews prune remains like cud.

Met with Pretty Sharma and she's looked at the Advance Care Form. According to the Advance Care Form if he's not well then he gets antibiotics but that's it. No feeding tube.

Pretty says that we should expect Dad's condition to fluctuate.

So he may be comatose for 3 days and then be quite lucid for a day, but then he might be comatose again...

Pretty asked if we'd want to keep him here or take him to hospital when the time comes?

Dad sleeping so soundly he couldn't be roused to ask if he wanted a coffee.

NOTES FOR COPING

Don't compare yourself to others.

You are doing your thing.

You are in your time, space and locality and that is it.

You are doing what you do.

Do what you do.

Don't worry about anything else.

The past and the future do not exist.

Now exists.

Live now.

Be here now.

It's okay.

Whatever happens it's okay.

Simply be.

You are human, and you experience the full gamut of emotions so just go with it.

Tap in to your larger "S" Self.

Don't anticipate.

Don't regret.

You wouldn't want to be them anyway.

You wouldn't want to be with them anyway.

You have transcended.

You are vibrating on a very high, and delicate, and volatile frequency now.

It's up to you to come to terms with all of this.

Write, write, write.

Write poetry.

Be poetic.

Learn from Michael and Ann Barbato about speaking, living and communicating via metaphor like Stephen Jenkinson does.

Don't be afraid to not explain yourself.

Stephen Jenkinson talks about the need to be able to make mistakes.

Be imperfect.

Be a work in progress.

Be okay with figuring it out and making mistakes along the way.

Be a mess.

Don't worry about other people.

No need to react to other people.

Say sorry and walk away.

Don't expect.

Everybody is doing their best.

No need to be offended.

Write your own story metaphorically, figuratively and real.

Be unbound.

Boundless love.

Love in all its forms.

Be in love with love.

Be in love with the blue sky, the shining sun, the rain, the greenery of the forest.

The everything.

It's all okay.

Meditate.

Sing, and play, and listen to music, and look after yourself, and simply be.

Live, and live well, and live graciously, and with great heart.

Be open.

Be open to all opportunities.

You do what you can, and you have done what you can, and that is all that you can do.

You are living in harmony.

When all else is dissonant the harmonious bell has even greater value and resonance.

Be the harmonious bell that you are.

Be open to all and have your own boundaries.

Be cool Dools.

THURSDAY 10 OCTOBER

Sleeping soundly in his dark room.

I got his porridge pre-emptively.

And then he roused because of his cough, so I raised the back of his bed up more to reduce the chance of coughing and then he woke. He asked:

"Are there any? Any um...anything...anything in a smidge?"

The nurse came to check on us and he said he wanted her to feed him instead of me.

I offered him his water bottle to help with his cough and he ignored me.

I'm not sure whether he uses his right hand anymore.

I asked:

"Do you use your right hand?"

The response was that there was no response. It was like he hadn't heard me. A blank "Pa stare" out into nothingness.

His next words were:

"That is delicious."

"This is really nice."

He finishes the first bowl and I ask:

"Do you want another bowl of porridge?"

And he says,

"That one will do."

So the nurse offers him some water but he rejects it and says,

"No, I'll just have some more porridge."

But he's just said no to more porridge but now says he does actually want more.

Loving the prunes!!!

Rick and Meg are visiting at lunchtime.

Bob Peacock is planning a birthday extravaganza for Dad tomorrow.

Carol Stirling coming at dinner time tonight.

I don't know about B. I haven't seen nor heard from her directly since April.

Very stern "No" to the question about doing any videos.

He's either disinterested or not happy about his Bday.

Definitely disinterested, other than in the lemon meringue pies and portuguese tarts that are coming with it.

It's official:

Today is a "3 Bowl Day!!!"

Bobby went past in his wheelchair and Dad said:

"You do well to pick his footprint."

And then,

"Anymore?" And we launch into porridge and prune round 3.

Scoreboard reads: PSLD - 3 : Bowls - nil

Listening to Herb Alpert and the Tijuana Brass playing Tijuana Taxi for his birthday.

He loved it.

And smashing bowl 3.

Dozing.

And a bit of a cough.

His care level has gone up because he doesn't seem to use his right hand anymore so can't drink by himself.

I'm giving a dying man his final wishes
Every day!

TUESDAY 15 OCTOBER

Sometimes I feel quite sick about the whole situation with Dad...

Sitting at Sydney Domestic Airport at sunrise, Tuesday 15 October

First memories of Dad:

Frozen with fear I'm calling out:

"Dad! Dad! Dad!"

Lying in the midst of a night terror and Dad comes in and lifts me up and carries me into the warm coziness of snuggling in between Dad and Mum.

In recent times Dad has been fearful of being alone and I've been able to return the favour of comforting him.

Dad had that Glioblastoma (GBM) in 2016, and, well and truly in 2017 when he brought 13 year old Nicola to WA for the first time and when he did his UK, Europe & Barbados trip.

Just now watching white, bright moon dance behind gentle moving soft clouds.

Sky brightening.

Moon hiding behind large white/grey cloud.

Thinking of my friend in his situation with his daughter and her eye cancer diagnosis.

Sparkling lights of Sydney International Terminal and the 12 storey carpark.

A giant Airbus A 330-200 on its giant landing gear wheels sits across to my left.

Gary Reynolds and I organised with Nic & Rheyse to book Rheyse's flights last night. One on my Virgin Frequent Flyer Velocity points returning on Sunday 26 January 2020, Australia Day.

I bought a Virgin Lounge Membership pass so all 3 of us could go in the Virgin Lounge together.

Moon bright, iridescent pearl
Gently appears,
Sails behind cloud again.
Pastel sunrise,
Morning star sparkling.
It too disappears behind a cloud,

Airport coming to life.

Silver Jetstar plane passes.
Powerful jet turbines whirring.
Orange, flashing lights of service vehicle driving across runways.
Businessmen in suits walk briskly to present their tickets while a high pitched "bip berp" sounds, then the next ticket "bip berp."

Businessmen going to Melbourne on business, and one blonde haired businesswoman, and a young Indian lady.

2 silver Jetstar planes cross in opposite directions.

Half a dozen more businessmen, and then 2 young women present their tickets: "bip berp" x 8 and I do feel a little woozy.

No. 1. Flight out for the day: "vrooooooom whoooirrrrrrrrrrrrrr" across and takes off – Big Emirates A 380 – will next be touching the ground in a v. different world in The Middle East in Dubai, UAE. The A330-200 that had been outside my window is being shifted by a transporter to the other side for the 9:30am flight to Perth. Another A 330-200 "Gnaraloo Bay" arrives to replace it.

Moon glowing glorious.

A heavy businessman arrives, his large protruding belly heaving as he huffs and puffs relieved he made it, followed by a cool, young guy who appears nonplussed despite their tight timeframe.

Orange, pinkish morning light hue touching International Terminal buildings as glass glows golden.

A woman arrives puffing, "sorry" as she hands the ticket officer her ticket to board, and the giant A 330-200 dispenses its passengers from Perth.

6:25am - We'll be boarding soon – actually that other A330 – 200 looks like it's at gate 42 for our flight at 7:15am.

THURSDAY 24 OCTOBER

I am thrown back.

So many pleasures and pains.

Overwhelm.

Overwhelmed.

I feel overwhelmed.

And I don't know what to do.

FRIDAY 25 OCTOBER

With Dad and his situation, it's like a baby, you don't abandon a little baby.

Sunday 27 October

He would tell our stories to everyone he met.

In my dream I am crying

In my dream I am crying as I think of my Father as a 6-year-old boy as Thich Nhat Hanh asks us to do.
I wake up, it's 6am Monday morning and I am crying.

MONDAY, 28 OCTOBER

Dad sleeping.

Warren W, resident that Phil and Abbey met, is sitting by the window. I walk up the corridor and read "Warren W" and "Ann W" on his room, and realise that it was his wife who died on Friday. He has advanced dementia and wanders aimlessly like a lost soul. The other day he mentioned to me how he was "just waiting for the lady of the house to come home." He always appears confused. Just now as he was wandering the hall we approached each other and he said, "The lady of the house. I'm not sure if she's sleeping or not?" Heartbreaking. And as we parted the salt water burned the insides of my nasal passages like being dumped by a massive breaker in the surf.

Dad keeps sleeping.

I overhear Bobby talking about how Warren doesn't remember that his wife has died because of his advanced Alzheimer's.

Dad not going v well.

Both arms heavily bandaged and arms are cold and bruised and mottled and bandaged.

Hardly uses right arm and hardly able to function it when does get it out.

Not in a good way at all.

Dozing 98% of time when not eating.

He kept repeating:

"How's the azeear?"

I didn't know what he meant and he couldn't communicate what he meant to me.

Significant dropping of left side of mouth.

Hardly spoke today.

It sounded like he was saying ASIO.

It took us five minutes to clarify that, in deed, that was exactly what he was asking.

I replied that I have no idea.

He is not in a good way.

TUESDAY 29 OCTOBER

Thinking about life with Dad, and caring for Dad, you have to go with how things are.

You have to be here now, and not be getting caught up in ideas of the past and memories etc.

It's simply a matter of being here now and attending this moment.

An old memory came up today of the bottle of Clayton's in the fridge door next to a bottle of Dry Ginger Ale.

LOOKING AT TRAIN BOOKS WITH WARREN

Warren W. and I looked at train pics in books for hours.

He's a huge train enthusiast.

It was hugely moving, being with this old man with advanced dementia who didn't remember that his wife had died. But there was something underlying. He had these flashes of real anger - right there. I was nearly in tears the whole time. It was such a privilege to be there with him in that time of grieving, even if it was sort of unconsciously for him...

WALKING ALONG NELSON BEACH UP TO PLANTATION POINT WHERE HE PLACED LUCY'S ASHES

Walking along Nelson Beach up to Plantation Point where he placed Lucy's ashes.

So much loss.

Never thought we would be here without him, because that never entered the equation, because we are a family, and our family was together, and this was the family holiday house.

But Mum and Dad will never come here again.

And maybe that's the whole point, it's certainly part of it.

They lived, and they lived here.

And they go on living in The Gracewood and at Quakers Hill Nursing Home.

And this place lives on in their memories, as they live on in ours.

And I'm overwhelmed by nostalgia, and grief, and longing, and loss.

And my daughter can't help me now.

Because everywhere I look is a place where I was with them pre-her.

And it's a loss that she does not know and cannot know now.

I suppose her time will come when I am in their place and she is in mine.

And the setting sun casts my shadow long.

And I face towards the west and the sun warms my face as I prepare to journey after it.

31 OCTOBER

The ending of things that were very "Dad" brings it all to the surface. The grief triggers are everywhere. My spellcheck just wanted to change "grief" to "fried" and I think that's pretty accurate. Everyone on the "Glioblastoma support page" says the same thing of the suffering for the patient, and their loved ones.

MESSAGE TO A FRIEND

Hi Lynnie,

I hope all's well for you and John.

Dad's condition can be seen to be worse every fortnight or so, but there are ups and downs. Some days he is more engaged than others. But, overall, when he's not eating, he's dozing most of the time. And, he doesn't speak as much. You're welcome to see him anytime. There are no plans for my brothers to be around.

All my love

ON COMPLETING THE MIDWIFING DYING COURSE

I have received support and guidance and encouragement during my father's very long dying year. And I don't know how I would have coped with the grief and aloneness and uncertainty without this course, particularly our time together in Kiama. I discovered that equally important to all the technical aspects regarding death and dying is the capacity to get in touch with myself. It's vital for the amicus to be connected to themselves.

FRIDAY 8 NOVEMBER

MY FATHER LIES INCREMENTALLY DYING FROM BRAIN CANCER.

His dying process has continued on for months longer than anybody had anticipated.

And yet each day is today and each day is now.

I have been reading and listening to a lot of Stephen Jenkinson's work.

It has been helpful.

And so I am here again, and my life is complicated, and I am in one piece.

The situation is very challenging and difficult.

The smell is overpowering.

I think it is partially from his infection - unfortunate smells.

I am somewhat disorganised this morning.

SUNDAY 10 NOVEMBER

I'm very disturbed and upset.

I need to keep practising the art of patience, and silence, and compassion, and self engagement, and living my life and not getting caught in the frames of other people.

MONDAY 11 NOVEMBER

You can be present, and simply be there.

You may not want to be there, and you may not feel it, but you are a healing presence.

Relax into that, and let all of the past worries, and hopes and fears, and challenges fade away.

Actively breathe, and expand your stomach and diaphragm out.

Nothing to do.

Nothing to achieve.

· · ·

Simply being with what is.

Peter has been struck down.

That is what has happened.

He has been struck down and he is suffering.

And when the merciful time of completion of his dying finally comes he will be released.

And he will be grateful.

The end of that will happen when it happens.

TUESDAY 12 NOVEMBER

Sleeping soundly late into breakfast time.

Dipa feeds him porridge.

He scrunches his forehead up.

Dipa and I ask him what's wrong.

And he scrunches his forehead up again.

He says, "More than anything..."

RN Jolie comes and checks on him. And the Centre Manager Jan Martin happens to be on the floor and comes to check on him at the same time.

They are very thorough with him and he expresses that he has no pain or concerns and wishes to continue eating his porridge.

Me: "You said, "more than anything?" What was it you wanted to say?"

Dad: "I don't know."

Dipa continues feeding him porridge.

He's a bit confused this morning. Maybe it's just some slight delirium. Plenty of "Pa stare" and almost like the rhythmic breathing of sleep, but while still receiving the spoon fulls from Dipa. With eyes closed much of the time or a somewhat confused look on his face.

Dipa feeds him second bowl.

Plenty of "Pa stare."

He had to be hand provided with his water by Dipa as he wasn't capable of getting water himself.

Although struggling he was able to tell me that he wanted a white coffee.

Voice very weak and high pitched.

Rhythmic breathing through nose.

Unable to activate right arm to get the coffee cup to drink, so I tried to spoon the coffee to him, but that was difficult so we agreed to try with a straw.

Straw seemed to work, but breathing almost like panting, but through the nose.

RN Jolie comes to check on him and he smiled at her, and she found that all his vital signs are ok.

He just seems a little bit delirious, and a bit not quite right this morning but the nurses are all aware of his condition and keeping a good eye on him.

Breathing very solidly through his nose as if he's asleep even when he's got his eyes open and people are talking to him.

IN MANY WAYS I HAVE ALWAYS BEEN...

In many ways I have always been an unsatisfied person.

In many ways I have been a restless person.

That is not the word I'm looking for though.

In many ways I have been an unsettled person.

But still not the word I'm looking for.

In many ways I have been an unable to sit happily with the status quo person.

. . .

Obviously not the words that I'm looking for, but tending to convey the meaning that I have.

There are all sorts of different types of people, and the contented people, if there are ones, do appear to be somewhat happier.

But is happiness the goal?

I think almost that what I was seeking to say was that I have always been a somewhat discontented person. I think that might have been what it was that I was getting at.

5:19AM FRIDAY 15 NOVEMBER

He will get sicker, and sicker, and there is nothing you can do about it.

Relax.

It might seem strange to say relax, but nevertheless relax.

Grieve, and stay connected with your higher self.

This is not an easy time for anybody, the least of all him.

But as you know from previous experiences with these types of times, the third force comes in to support him, and you, and everyone.

So hold onto the thread.

It is your vital source, and you are enough, and have enough.

Be.

Be.

Be here now.

These many languages.

Voices speaking.

Including the languages of the different birds.

Birdsong.

The distant crow cawing out.

Now smothered by the traffic.

We wait in line for our opportunity.

We wait in line.

Partially in sun.

And we shuffle into the darkness.

Overseen by security dangling their keys.

PREPARATIONS FOR THE VISITORS (AT THE TIME OF THE THINNING OF THE VEIL)

Be prepared for the visitors to come to Dad to journey with him beyond this corporeal form.

I HAVE DONE MY BEST TO BE AS GOOD TO THE MAN AS POSSIBLE

I have done my best to be as good to the man as possible.

This has been according to my own standards, and I know that they are not the standards of all.

Yet it is my best, and they are my standards, and those are the circumstances under which he and I have always engaged.

We have influenced each other no doubt, and yet we have been, and remain very much our own individuals.

And this is where the tears come.

He is now in a state of extreme incapacity.

Something that he never could have, or would have imagined for himself.

And so what am I to do?

And I don't know, and haven't known what to do.

I have been feeling my way in the dark, stubbing my toe, stumbling at times tripping
over and knocking over precious items that break.

Apparently some people who have not spoken to me, have told others their criticisms of my ways, and put forward their arguments against me, including some allegations of unconventionality. During this whole period nobody has approached me with any criticisms, complaints, or arguments other than X right at the beginning at the time of the first operation in October 2017, and subsequently when screaming at me in April 2019.

As of this writing it is Saturday morning 16 November 2019, the eve of my brother Phil's 50th birthday and Peter continues to lie immobile in his extremely weakened, and compromised state in his bed at the Gracewood.

Never again will he see a sunset, or a sunrise, and he hasn't asked to see one either.

Never again will he walk his dog.

He loved walking his dog.

Pain in the pit of my stomach.

Pain of his loss.

Pain as he cast his dogs ashes into the bay at their favourite point.

Never again will he stand.

That's a pretty simple thing isn't it?

But never again will he stand.

Never again will he stand, and that must grieve him sorely.

Having been so much.

And now to be so diminished physically.

He has felt all this acutely.

And so you must too.

I do.

And I am.

HERE WITH DAD WHILE HE IS DYING FROM BRAIN CANCER

Here with Dad while he is dying from brain cancer.

He lays there with his eyes closed, and his mouth open breathing heavily.

Soon he will disappear from this form.

Very hard to bear.

But these are truths that come no matter how we may feel about them.

"Such is life."

And so we are here.

Dad laying back on his bed.

Mouth wide open.

Almost panting for breath with his challenged breathing.

I followed up the RN, the male nurse, H and he said that Dr B hasn't seen Dad for a week and he'll organise for Dad to hopefully see Dr B this Monday 18 November.

SMOKED OUT

To top everything off the smoke alarm went off right in the middle of a dream, in the middle of the night, last night.

The smoke alarm was activated by bushfire smoke far away, but nevertheless its intense high octane decibel screeching tore me from my nightly slumber like an unprepared infant torn from the womb.

Needless to say my umbilical cord was ripped.

We receive what the people who lived before us left. For instance, I am driving the car that Dad chose based on what he wanted. His preferences and his choice.

The world that we inhabit has been being created for tens of thousands of years by its inhabitants, whether they be human, animal, plant, fungus, or otherwise.

Just like me driving my Dad's car we receive the earth as a vehicle that we are riding.

And so we have a choice as to whether we turn on the ignition and drive the car, and we choose whether to drive on a certain road, or in a particular direction, but we have no control over the choices that were made before us, for example as to what type of car, or other vehicle to obtain.

We also have no choices as to the concept, and design, and manufacture of the vehicle itself.

Right now I'm turning at the corner of Gilbert Road, on Showground Road, where I once ploughed Dad's blue Magna wagon into the gutter because it under steered.

It was a real shock to me at the time.

I was driving with Chuck.

Dad came and sorted everything out and was okay about it.

I felt terrible.

But Dad understood that accidents happen.

We were a family for a period of time.

Now things are somewhat distanced.

And on this morning I am driving along Showground Road, past Victoria Avenue, and about to turn right onto Windsor Road on my way to see Dad in the Gracewood once again.

It is a difficult time for all of us, not the least of which for Dad, and just like the choices of the cars in the world that are left to us, we have no choice as to the disease that Dad is suffering from.

He has the brain cancer, and it is slowly progressing in its growth and subsequent impacts on his brain, and body, and capacity.

His capacity is now very limited.

Someone said to me yesterday something along the lines of the fact that they'd already given Dad up.

This is what Stephen Jenkinson says that the healthy people do in relation to the dying people.

The healthy people treat the dying people as no longer relevant when they still have life coursing through them.

So we must be there with all of the living, as Michael Barbato changed the name of his book to "Being with the living and the dying."

We must be there with those who are dying in a way that recognises, and engages with the fact that, until after they have died they continue to be 100% alive. Because you are either dead or alive. You are not in between, and so, if someone is dying that means they are not dead.

And that means they are alive, and that means they need everything that a living person needs, whether they can feel anything, or are conscious of anything, or are unresponsive.

There are certain people that seem to inherently know this, and then there are others who give up the people who are still living.

MONDAY 18 NOVEMBER

Catching the 4:49am 400 Bus to Sydney Airport.

5:12am Heaps of people get in at the Randwick stop, including a full-sized pram with baby in it, and the baby's two parents.

They lift, and push the pram, to fit in front of the suitcase of the young Chinese guy that got on with me at Bondi Junction.

5:14am And we are now a fully crowded Sydney public transport squish burger!!! How much would it have been for me to catch that Uber the whole way to the airport?

5:15am Heaps more people getting on, including people with suitcases for the airport.

They squeeze past us.

It's getting light outside.

A beautiful mauve hue, and lightly playing a recording of a woman's voice singing:

"Trees of green
Red roses too
What a wonderful world"

And the bus rattles on at the fastest possible speed.

Engine whirring, and everything on board shaking.

Now the ladies voice sings:

"Twinkle twinkle little star," and I remember how this was one of Nic's favourite songs.

And I'm taken back.

And it was good.

5:32am and streams of traffic are pouring in both directions.

White light one way.

Red light the other way.

Sydney is fully awake, even if me and most of my fellow travellers are not.

I'm carrying my Dad's brown leather jacket with me - the one he wore so much.

He often looked a little tired or something in it.

I can't remember seeing him actually lay down and rest, not in front of the TV or with a book or the paper very often, but I can remember this one time when he lay back on a banana chair and slept outside in the garden at Dural. Somehow that really touched me, the way he really slept and appeared to be really relaxing there.

And now I'm carrying that brown coat of his across the country.

I've carried it through the night and now I'm carrying it across the country.

Clear on take off, but then significant smokey haze from bushfires from the north and west, and maybe the south.

Then at the foot of the Blue Mountains the haze becomes so strong as to almost make it opaque.

Very thick bushfire smoke.

Late afternoon: W.A. South-West Highway Puma Service Station:

Billy Joel, *"It's all about Soul."*

URGENT RETURN MESSAGE TO MY BROTHERS

Pretty Sharma the level 2 manager has just phoned me and told me that Dad appears to be in the actively dying phase. And has not been on antibiotics for some days now.

I am currently urgently re-arranging things and will be flying into Sydney on Qantas at 9pm tonight.

Pretty told me that she has contacted me as soon as she noticed a change in Dad's condition. She said it is a change from yesterday. She said he looks comfortable but he's more sleepy than yesterday. She said he just opened his eyes a little bit today. She said that if he's not fully waking up then they won't be able to get the antibiotics into him now. She said that if we give him antibiotics we will prolong things. I asked Pretty to contact each of you directly to ensure that you can enquire with her directly about everything.

Let me know if there's anything you need from me.

DREAM - FRIDAY 22 NOVEMBER

Friday, 22 November 2019 with Dad in the Gracewood after I raced back with Qantas yesterday.

Woke up having had a dream in which my mobile phone has dropped and has a hairline crack.

The next thing I looked down and the glass of the iPhone screen is all broken and seems to be breaking further.

My understanding of the dream is that it is reminiscent of Dad's body, and the way that his body is, and appears to have a hairline fracture but he's actually disintegrating.

Pretty serious stuff.

Upsetting.

I couldn't understand why I couldn't put the phone together, or what happened to it.

SATURDAY 23 NOVEMBER ("MIRACLE SATURDAY")

Lying in bed sleeping, and appearing quite peaceful, except for when coughing and face screws up.

Not on oxygen.

Dry coughing.

I'm preparing everything and then suddenly.

Eyes wide open and wide awake.

"Good morning."

"Good morning."

And he's chatty as if nothing's happened.

RN Jolie prepares to assess him.

We get him thickened water, and porridge with prune juice.

And he's chatty.

Eyes wide open.

Jolie amazed at his alertness.

Tried FaceTiming Chuck.

FaceTimed with Phil and he wished Phil "Happy Birthday" – a miracle.

Tried video, but he doesn't seem to relate well with devices and flat 2 D screens anymore.

An extraordinary morning - "The Miracle on 2 Free Settlers Drive Street"

Nurse Miriam comes and gives him his meds, and is very excited to see him and comments on how he is fully alert today.

Nurse Anoma came and chatted with him, and he gave her a big smile.

RN Jolie had brought him some strawberry yoghurt, but he didn't want any of that. He's all about the porridge and prune juice.

Carolyn and Nicola visited.

I go to bed as early as possible, with the lights down low, and some good books to read and the candles on.

The alarms are set, including the clock radio emergency alarm.

The morning apple is ready to eat on the way to the Gracewood.

IT'S NOT A GOOD STATE OF AFFAIRS

It's not a good state of affairs. He is not well and he is continuing to struggle.

He is not coping.

I am not coping.

The family is not coping.

Nobody is coping.

She is not coping.

It takes a lot out of me hosting all of those people, and organising everything.

And our latest visitor is just another person to host, and to organise, and to keep informed.

It's all very frustrating, and annoying, and exhausting, and difficult, and hard, and painful, and upsetting, and all the rest.

But what do you do?

I don't know, we just keep on doing what we've been doing I suppose.

SUNDAY 24 NOVEMBER

Still trying to make sense of Dad's situation.

I suppose it's like trying to feel my way in the dark with lots of holes in the ground.

It's something you have to feel your way through, and most likely will always be in one way or the other.

The cockatoos are screeching in the night.

IN THE TEMPLE

People here are called residents, not patients. But there's the dead give away right there. When was the last time someone called you a "resident?" Probably only if it was a politician trying to sell you something based on false promises of "community."

It's a temple to the God of Infirmity.

Nobody would be in here if they could avoid it.

It's their incapacity that lands them in here, and keeps them here.

Captive to their own failing bodies.

This is a place of last resort. A place of struggling against the landslip of the falling apart of the body. The thing about this place is that none of the residents "stroll." They shamble, and push their walkers, ride in various wheeled contraptions, but they don't stroll 'cause if they could stroll they wouldn't be here!

BEING IN THE HOUSE

Being in the house is difficult, but ultimately helps with the grieving process because you see everything every day, and the changes seep into you slowly and gradually, but surely.

The absences are felt every day.

And every day, as that absence is felt, you slowly, and gradually, like the sun moving through the course of the day, become accustomed to the changes.

It is painful, and it is not easy, but it is an experience that has to be gone through.

Every single one of those little reminders is both a pain imposing event, and concomitantly, a salve.

And so I slowly experience, and come to terms with, the grief and loss, and the change and the finality of it all, as we lead into Christmas, and potentially the first Christmas after he has gone.

He was not around last Christmas either but he was still alive.

He was having Christmas with Chuck and Jenny, and Caitlin and Alicia in California, and we Facetimed.

At that time he was coming back, but now he will never be coming back.

And the chairs will remain empty, and his room will remain empty, and his bed will remain empty, and the house will remain empty, and none of the family events that happened before will happen again in the same way, or potentially at all.

And this is a painful realisation, and one that cannot be overcome, but has to be experienced.

This is grief.

This is life.

This is loss.

This is the human experience.

This is not easy.

This is the way that it is.

You're gonna have to find ways of living with that son.

MONDAY 25 NOVEMBER

He has a cough that he can't get rid of.

Repeatedly trying to clear his throat without avail.

I bring Nurse Anoma to him.

And also liaise with RN H but he's not the RN for our floor today and then male Nurse Nagib comes to give him his meds.

The cough is terrible.

In a bad way with the cough.

RN Shamila is called.

I've been told by them that the gurgling in the throat and lungs isn't good.

Responsive to RNs and Kerry from Client Liaison.

Given an injection of a small dose of Robinol to ease the irritation.

His porridge etc was brought in but everyone decided it was best not to proceed after about 2 mouthfuls as there was too much of a risk of aspiration.

Constantly trying to clear the throat.

The RNs and Kerry said they'll notify all staff to keep him more upright overnight.

The Gracewood Manager, Jan Martin came and checked on him.

Cough still there but not as constant as the Robinol and sitting upright takes effect, but still a sort of growl, gurgle sound, and still a lot of coughing.

Pretty Sharma recommends bringing the Palliative Care Expert from Westmead back in to see Dad.

Went down to ground floor and visited Karen of the Cumberland Cafe as 1927's "If I could" plays on the radio.

Visited Leslie on level 1.

Still has gurgly throat and cough.

11:45am Hadn't eaten any porridge so we tried some porridge.

V slowly having small mouthfuls of porridge.

V bad gurgly cough.

V bad gurgling like a drain and difficult cough.

I stopped feeding him porridge because the gurgling was too disconcerting.

A tough day for all.

Nurse Kim feeds him lunch.

More gurgly, and more coughing after lunch.

Loved the reading from Golf and The Spirit.

Lyn Archibald came and visited and it was good to receive her wisdom as an experienced Nurse and Nursing Trainer.

Lyn recommends drying the secretions with something like the Robinol, and keep him elevated to drain it.

She asked if he's on fluid tablets.

She noticed his oedemas.

That gurgly cough is bad.

But overall within all of this he's been more responsive today than you'd think.

Kim spoke with RN Shamila to find out when he can have his next Robinol.

Shamila looked at him a bit before 2pm and thought it's best to wait until later with the Robinol.

It does dry you up and that gives you other problems so they'll just keep monitoring him.

Kerry came again and we read poetry to him.

TUESDAY 26 NOVEMBER 2019
GRACEWOOD BAPTISTCARE KELLYVILLE

Sleeping, but regular sound of painfully trying to clear throat.

Woah! Confronting - not good this morning.

Face very red and flushed.

Spoke to Anoma.

RN Jolie came and looked at him and assessed the flushed red face.

He's generally hot.

Very out of it.

RN Jolie checks temperature.

9:10am Getting to the end of the time when we can feed him - just got the porridge before they were going to say it had been there too long and was being thrown out.

So we try to feed him porridge and prune juice.

Not good at all this morning.

V bad gurgling and cough.

RN Jolie and the nurse gave him a swab with the Oraswab for oral care.

Tried to say something incomprehensible.

RN Jolie said to feed him his thickened water through a spoon first before feeding him his porridge.

Things have slowed markedly.

V difficult morning.

Ate some porridge with prune juice.

Strange guttural sound in throat and a bit of moaning.

Very unresponsive and immobile today. Propped with head up and forward like a puppet - such a disconcerting state. Equal to or more so than "Pa stare."

Face still red. I don't think it's just from the pillow like RN Jolie was suggesting.

Exhausted.

I go and see RN Jolie again about his red, hot flushed face and I ask for Dr B to come and look at it.

Big gurgly cough like a drain.

Just opening left eye at the moment, and it seems to kind of stay open and rolled back while sleeping or "Pa staring." Neck very stiff, and kind of stuck in place, and neither I nor Nurse Kim could adjust him at all.

Moaning. Not sure if he's trying to speak or just weakly trying to clear his throat.

Don't know if we'll see another lucid, chatty morning like the Saturday morning we just had...

Pretty Sharma says that the redness in his right cheek may be from his body being unable to regulate heat.

But RN Jolie says core temp is ok.

EXPECTATIONS

Expectations are a big thing.

We all expect so much from each other.

I need to learn to relax, and expect less from others, while understanding that they will still expect a lot from me.

SUPPORTING EACH OTHER IN THE TIME OF DYING

The times that I've raced back from Perth to Sydney this year haven't been just for Dad.

They've been to be with and support the other people with Dad:

- Chuck

- Nurses and Care Staff

- Friends and relatives

- Etc

There are many people involved in the dying of a person, and often the dying person is not the one who needs the most support.

SLOWED

I've slowed down a lot with doing this for Dad.

It slows you down.

We change based on the circumstances that we are in.

His state of being is extremely reduced and slowed now.

As he would say, almost to a snail's pace.

IN AMONGST IT ALL, THIS

I don't think you ever really get over not living with your child.

There's a kind of anticipation and loving experience that happens.

And then that's torn away, and at various times you're filled with such overpowering memories, and longing that you don't know what to do with yourself.

THURSDAY 28 NOVEMBER

Sleeping.

B visited again last night but I don't think she's visiting today. Carol's visiting tonight.

Ruby feeds him porridge.

Right eye still stuck shut from infection.

I ask Ruby if someone can put some cream on his right eye.

She says that Dr B has written a script and they'll be putting chlorsig eye drops on it when the chlorsig arrives from the pharmacy.

Silently receives porridge into mouth. The eeriness of his being conscious and even having his eyes open and staring at me but never ever saying a word. When this goes on, and on, it is very unnerving.

Right cheek is no longer inflamed.

Something gets caught, or something, and he suffers a tremendous cough endeavouring to shift the obstruction.

I had left my Kindle with M Scott Peck's "Golf and The Spirit" home charging so I read to him from Thomas Moore's "The Guru of Golf" and he loved it. His eyes tracked, and locked on me, while I read it and Ruby kept feeding him porridge and thickened water.

Has a bit of a cough coming up, probably as a result of having eaten.

IT'S VERY DIFFICULT BUT YOU HAVE TO LET THE GRIEF WASH RIGHT THROUGH YOU

It's very difficult but you have to let the grief wash right through you.

I go in and see him every day, first thing.

My brothers are both OS so there's few others on the ground here to really make a substantial difference.

But what do you do?

You just keep going...

FRIDAY 29 NOVEMBER

Sleeping but v bad cough this morning. Miriam said she was v upset because Dad had been left lying flat overnight and this has exacerbated his cough.

A patient (they call them residents, but they're actually patients) on level 2 is repeatedly screaming, and making it hard to think about anything else.

Dad's gurgly cough is extremely bad this morning.

Like a blocked drain - gurgling up but not being fixed.

Q. Whether he should have any breakfast due to the stuff already in there?

I was also wondering if Ashley his masseuse has been around, so I contacted her boss, Su-Gai Hood at A Touch of Wellbeing to find out, and Su-Gai said they'll arrange for Ashley to see him again.

RN Anita comes with some porridge to see how he goes. First feeds him some water via a spoon. He opens his eyes and then closes them again, and then coughs harshly. RN Anita suggests another drink and says:

"See how we go."

And he repeats:

"Yeah, we'll see how we go."

Anita offers him porridge and he opens his eyes for a sec and receives the porridge.

Anita says he had a v good dinner yesterday.

He starts coughing, and trying to clear the obstruction again.

He had slid right down since originally being placed in the bed, and his feet are off the end of the bed.

Adjusted by being slid up to the head of the bed, so that he's more upright and his chest can clear better.

RN Anita tests his capacity to drink, and unfortunately he coughs too much, and so we decide to hold off feeding him this morning.

And we have him as upright as possible to clear the stuff that's caught in his throat and chest.

Gurgly sound in throat and trouble clearing it.

9:30am Anita returned and tried him with more thickened

water, and then when that was ok she fed him some porridge. He had some, but then after a while started coughing again so Anita swapped the porridge over for more thickened water.

Big gurgly sound and cough.

Overall peaceful and sleeping and restful.

SATURDAY 30 NOVEMBER

Eyes open and I think we are going to have another Miracle Saturday, but no such luck - no comment. Just greeted by a Pa stare - a v imposing way to start the day. I won't say it didn't give me a wobble. Nothing said by him, just the stare, a flicker of the eyelids and then closed. And that was that.

Followed a little later by a loud clearing of the throat.

Significant gurgly cough.

Least engaged day.

Very silent.

Not much coughing.

Miriam agreed and said he's v sleepy.

Not much else to report.

SUNDAY 1 DECEMBER 2019

Sleeping.

Has gurgle, and cough, and has a very strained expression as he struggles with the harsh, dry coughing.

I seek out a nurse to find if there's anything that can be done for his coughing.

Tested by RN Jolie, and approved for porridge, so porridge it is.

Even though as upright as possible some significant coughing.

That cough is not good.

Playing music CDs.

I haven't heard him say a word for what seems like days. Certainly no clear, full engagement like Saturday a week ago.

Big, gurgly throaty sound and cough.

Eyes closed most of the time, and when eyes open mainly "Pa stare" - The never speaking is very unnerving, and, combined with the "Pa stare" puts together a formidable combo.

I saw B as I was leaving today.

We had a chat and she told me how last Wednesday night she was joking with him and said how he saved it all up just so that she can feed him and then he responded with "possibly."

And she felt that was very much Peter, very much still there, and is still engaging with her.

Very painful stuff.

MONDAY 2 DECEMBER

Sleeping. And not much more to it really. Just, sleeping, the whole time, without disturbance.

Woke him at 9:15 to try to give him thickened water and then the porridge.

Feeding him porridge.

Nurse comes in with his medications.

Suddenly speaks up with his gravelly voice:

"Hello Maria."

Took me by absolute surprise - I haven't heard him speak for days.

He says:

"No thanks."

She says "No Panadol?"

He nods.

She says.

"No medications?"

He replies "No."

She didn't argue and then departed to return later.

Other than that he didn't say a word.

Just staring but did not say another word other than the exchange with Maria.

Most peculiar 😕

Ate all porridge.

TUESDAY 3 DECEMBER

Sleeping.

But although he's sleeping all the time he does appear peaceful.

Opened his eyes and "Pa stared" directly at me - very unnerving.

I spoke to him:

"Good morning!"

No reply. Nothing, nada, niet.

The most exciting thing this morning was the cleaner down on his hands and knees just outside the room trying to get at some hell of a disaster stain caused by God knows what, and I don't wanna know - vroom vroom vroom.

The vacuum cleaner working over time.

RN Jolie comes and Dad opens his eyes with a sour expression on his face.

She tests him and says he's ok to eat.

Rae, one of the residents, tries to negotiate the mess and says, "I can straddle it just about."

Bad cough after only 2 or 3 spoons of porridge.

Not good in ways that cannot be expressed in words.

Strange noises coming out of him after just a small amount of porridge.

RN Jolie checks him but finds that he's ok because the noise was him nasal breathing so he's good to keep eating.

V slow with eating and food sitting in mouth.

Sooooo slow.

Generally not a good morning.

Subtle shift - not in a good way...inexplicable in words.

In the room next door the old lady repeatedly calls out:

"Help me."

"Help me please."

"Please help me."

She was moved to that room because the residents up the other end had complained so much about her constantly calling out "help me."

And she does this continually, all day, every day.

Max Boys visited Dad today and Dad was quite cognisant and engaged with him. Max said that Dad loved the golf readings. He really responded to that. Max was surprised and happy that he was able to engage with Dad.

WEDNESDAY 4 DECEMBER

Sleeping. The nurses say he had a good, big dinner last night.

I watch videos of Arnold and Amy Mindell teaching about people in "Non-ordinary States of Consciousness."

Nurse Kim said that when she checked Dad at 6:30am he was coughing a lot. But for the hours that I've been here he hasn't coughed, or moved at all. Just rhythmic breathing of deep sleep.

9:35am Finally something: face screwed up and a harsh cough.

Raised him right up to drink and eat but no reaction.

Unable to be roused from sleeping.

THURSDAY 5 DECEMBER

Sleeping.

Suffering from an annoying cough that comes back.

And so I let Kim know, and I go and get RN Ruby and Miriam to come and look at him.

A lot of mucus coming out of his nose, and eyes flickering a lot like REM.

I let Miriam know, and she calls RN Nurse Ruby, who comes and looks at, and deals with, the mucus coming out of his nose, and goes away.

He doesn't stir.

RN Ruby comes back to check Dad, and to move him with Kim.

No stirring all day. Completely unresponsive all morn.

Opens mouth for spoon of thickened water from Ruby.

Tried to say something but just gurgly sound.

Tried again but just gurgle.

Then big gurgly cough.

Ruby continues with the water.

More gurgly coughing.

Trouble with it all.

Eyes flickering a lot like REM.

Ruby decides not to feed him and to leave it an hour and bring him water later.

She goes to get something for his eyes.

He coughs some more.

Sleeping.

Has large gurgly cough rumble up.

Ruby returns and attends to his eyes, and his face screws right up while she does that.

More rough gurgly cough.

No breakfast. Yesterday he had a big dinner.

Ashley from A Touch of Wellbeing is here and is going to give him his massage today.

Carol is coming in to see him this evening.

It appears that things have changed, but I could be wrong and things could change again, as could be seen from his interaction with Max Boys the other day. His needs have become less. He appears comfortable and relatively peaceful. Everything he needs must be done for him now. The only thing that he really actively does is cough, and I suppose you could even query whether that's activated by parts of the body that don't require volition to be activated.

People certainly aren't going to be wanting to come in here expecting/needing any responses from him...

He's been pretty much unresponsive the whole day.

B came in today.

Carol has come in tonight and he's more awake but not speaking. He's eaten all his dinner.

Carol will be returning again on Saturday.

IF HE WAS CONSCIOUS

If he was conscious and I was able to take him around in his chair then I would be doing that.

But he is not, so I can't, and so I sigh and I wonder, and I'm struggling, and I feel depressed and hopeless, and like I'm sliding backwards, scrabbling on a shifting rock heap that is slowly devouring me.

HE IS SLEEPING AS HE PREPARES HIMSELF TO GO ON A LONG JOURNEY

He is sleeping as he prepares himself to go on a long journey.

Simply be there for him, to help sustain him, to prepare him for his long journey. Others will do the same for you.

He is losing a lot, and is naturally concerned about that, and so he is learning now about how to prepare to go to the next level.

It is not unlike a video game.

He is going to do okay on his journey, but he does not know that now, and so you are simply there at the way station helping him as he deals with the nerves before going onto the stage.

You have done it, you can do it, he can do it too.

There is nothing to be afraid of.

Your own acculturated emotions have put you in a certain position but you can let that go now.

You can simply be and that is okay.

So be there for him and relax.

Relax.

There is nothing at all to worry about.

He is fine.

He is supported.

You have engaged within the ordinary state of consciousness enough, and you, and he, and everybody can all let it go now.

Just relax.

Sure, have the grieving experience.

And at the same time understand that you, and he, and everyone, are supported, and that there is nothing at all to worry about.

YOU ARE HOLDING VIGIL NOW FOR HIM

You are holding vigil now for him and that is important, and part of the whole process.

Sit with him, and be with that, and that is all you need.

No need to stress out, or require any responses, or anything like that.

Now is the time to be grateful to him, and for the journey that you've both been on together, as he prepares to launch.

It's all part of it.

You are supported.

. . .

It's time to let go, and let him go.

Relax.

FRIDAY 6 DECEMBER

Gurgly cough, and mucus around mouth while sleeping this morning.

Chatted with RN and he commented on Dad not being very alert, and that it's best not to try to force feed Dad when he's unresponsive because of the risk of aspiration. He said that Dad is often more alert at lunch and dinner times, and to feed him then.

We didn't disturb him this morning.

Slept right through the morning.

Occasional attempts at trying to clear throat while sleeping.

Not much else to report.

Liz Johnston seeing Dad at 2pm today.

Nic might come in with me to see him this arvo.

Carol is seeing him tomorrow (Saturday).

Dad's hands and feet are so swollen by the retention of lymph fluid that they're like grotesque puppet limbs. I find it so hard to see this and often have to look away.

I read to him, and to myself, John O'Donohue's "Entering Death", "For the Dying," and "Blessing to those who suffer."

THERE IS NO DOUBT

There is no doubt that Dad's sickness, and suffering, and dying, and ultimately his days, are very sad and tragic.

And although we may shy away from these truths, it is important to acknowledge them, and to know them for real.

Some people don't come in to see Dad, because emotionally they can't handle it, and they want to "remember him how he was."

I think there's a saying from the Bible that goes something along the lines of, "there is a friend who sticks closer than a brother," and that is what sick, and suffering, and dying people need.

We certainly don't need more people who won't be loving the sick, suffering, and dying person, because "I'd like to remember them how they were."

And so I come back to remembering how Dad was as he moved

around his life, always with purpose doing the things that he was doing.

He was a very strong, healthy, active, engaged, social man, and for somebody like that to get sick, and diminish, and no longer fill those spaces is quite confronting.

And we now talk of those times, as I did, and it was because he was a strong, active man, and he did do many things, but now he is lying immobile in his deathbed, slowly dying, and suffering.

He is certainly not taking to this experience with a lightness.

There was always a density, and a heaviness in his step.

And he continues to stoically grit his teeth, and bear the pain, and the suffering, and the loss of independence.

He was always a very proud, and self-contained, and self assured person, and he no longer has that.

And he has had this Glioblastoma for much longer than we would've thought.

They say that it probably begins about seven years before you are diagnosed with it.

He was diagnosed with this at the beginning of October 2017 which means he most likely had the beginnings of it, and was living with it, as it grew, from about 2010.

To put that in perspective it was before I met Lucinda.

So Lucinda, and the Giblett family, never knew him without the brain tumour, or at least the Glioblastoma. The last time that Dad visited Manjimup Nic Giblett commented on how he didn't seem himself to her and in hindsight that was clearly because he was suffering the effects of the Glioblastoma.

How were any of us to know?

And being something within the brain, it seems difficult for the brain to turn in and comprehend issues within itself.

And so all we can say was that Pete seemed a little off.

And I certainly found that he was repeating stories to me, but a lot of people do that.

But he suffered, and that's something to remember, and to always remember, and to not shy away from, but to allow to seep into you, and maybe even break you open a little more, or a lot, depending on your capacity.

As my brother Chuck's wife said to me back in about February, "it sucks," and that is a very apt description of the situation.

SATURDAY 7 DECEMBER

Sleeping very soundly on his side.

No cough, and no cough reported.

A little bit of a cough.

Carol is coming in later today.

Ruby feeding Dad some thickened water in a spoon and a tiny bit of porridge. Mainly just a little thickened water. Soooooooo slow. All in such slow motion with delayed reactions.

Couldn't really get him to open his mouth for the porridge - just the thickened water.

Not much.

Ruby left him with it to come back later.

Quite slumped down in his bed, so they'll slide him back up the bed.

They come and wash, and change him, and Anoma shaves him.

Sleeping soundly.

Not eating or drinking much today, but ate a full dinner last night.

Text to Carol at 6:30pm:

"Thanks Carol, Nicola and I are with him now and have noticed his shaking as well, and he indicated to us that it was from the cold. He didn't seem very happy, but he does seem a lot more relaxed now with Nic reading to him.
Thanks again and you have a good night too
x"

Nicola read to him William Stafford's "The Way It Is."

MY PARENTS ARE HUMAN

My parents are human, with all of the faults and frailties that human beings suffer from.

Many of Mum's challenges are well known.

Dad's challenges are less known.

Nicola was telling me how Dad's friend B was telling Nic that Dad had told B that he is not ready to go yet.

B had said to Peter, "Are you ready to go? To let go?"

And Peter had replied in a very strong and powerful and gruff manner "No."

. . .

So Dad has held a lot in throughout our whole lives.

John Hackwell has talked to me about me being someone who has known my father, but I don't know about that so much, because there is so much that, for whatever reason, he never shared.

In many ways he continued on stoically, and didn't share what was happening for him.

Obviously there is no obligation on anybody to share what's happening for them, but as a family member it's difficult when another family member holds so much back from sharing.

And this was a culture within our family.

If there was something that Mum didn't want to talk about, then she would just stand up and say, "I don't want to talk about that Simon. I don't want to talk about that Simon," and walk out of the room.

Dad was a different story because he was always very affable, and sociable, and quick with puns, and joking with people, but a bit like that friend of mine who described what Mel Gibson was like, in that he was very charming but you got the feeling that you never really got to know him.

. . .

And so there is a lot of Dad's private life that he has kept private, and that's fair enough, but it is difficult. And it's difficult to help someone who has always held back and continues to hold back.

All you can do is your best, but when that person, through a lifetime of habit, holds themselves to themselves, then you are stymied from being able to be there, for and with them.

And so he closes his eyes and he sticks it out.

And he gives me that baleful stare and I don't know what's going on when that is happening.

It's tough.

It's tough for him, and it's tough for me, and it's difficult for Nicola. Nicola gives him so much, and Nicola gives him so much that I could never provide.

But really the point of what I'm saying is that he's always held himself to himself, and people have to come willingly to the table, and if they don't then you can't force them to engage, but it is hurtful and difficult, and challenging, and it leaves you wondering.

. . .

It leaves you exhausted.

Because you are out in the cold. And that is where you begin to feel, and recognise the heat of your soul as that is all you have.

DAD ALWAYS HAD THE MOST EXCELLENT OF HEALTH

Dad always had the most excellent of health.

He was a light sleeper and he would awaken in the morning and never sleep in.

He would jump out of bed, and do his exercises, and get into his day and attend to one thing after the other without failing.

He had an extremely strong fortitude.

I on the other hand suffered, from a very early age, from all sorts of illnesses, and ailments, and allergies and rashes.

I suffered, and I lacked physical capacity.

I was an exceptionally deep sleeper, and I would go into a virtual coma state of a morning.

I have low blood pressure, and also get low blood sugar, resulting in me going into a virtual coma state.

I always needed to set an alarm, because I would always sleep in for hours, and hours, and hours, and Dad was always amazed by this, and would make the occasional comment.

Having never suffered in that way he didn't understand.

I'm sure he does now.

And so, perhaps inside of all this, it is apt, and fitting, that I as one who has suffered, and been incapable of getting out of bed, have been the one to be with him at this time when he is completely incapable of getting out of bed, or engaging in all of that movement that he both loved, and as one who has always been fit, and healthy, and capable, to some extent took for granted.

He was a strong man, not in the sense of an Arnold Schwarzenegger bodybuilder, but in his capacity to just keep on going.

He was, and even to this day, Sunday 8 December 2019, continues to be stoic.

He was a sportsman in every sense of the word, and loved to play cricket and golf.

In his early life he played other sports and did a lot of running.

In his early life he loved playing soccer and also cricket.

He loved watching many sports on the television, especially golf and rugby league, and cricket.

A memory that I will always have is of Dad sitting in his

reclining lounge chair with the remote control and watching the golf and switching over to the rugby league.

One thing that we really loved doing together was watching the sitcom Seinfeld.

Those stories always engaged us and gave us a good laugh.

That was certainly a space where we truly came together.

He was extremely impartial and was very supportive of each of us three boys in each of our endeavours.

He didn't directly talk to us much about these things, but we would hear from other people about all the stories that he had told them about all of the things that each of the three of us were doing that he found so compelling, and interesting, and of which he was so proud.

Robert Stanton commented on how in many ways Dad was a simple man.

And that is right.

He was an intelligent man who knew what he liked.

Like many others of his generation, in many ways, I suppose he was a man of his generation.

He enjoyed the music, and the tastes, and the food, and the interests, and the travel, and the people, and the sport, and predilections of his particular generation.

Towards the end, when the brain tumour was really biting,

certain difficult aspects of his personality definitely came out, and his views were parting further away from those held by me and my daughter Nicola. For instance at the time that the gay marriage plebiscite to vote to allow gay marriage was coming through he would simply make jokes with Nicola and I about it without ever being prepared to get into a proper discussion about it. We have no doubt that he voted against gay marriage. But it was not something that he was prepared to have a proper discussion with us about. And that was the case with many, many things. He just wasn't interested in that kind of stuff. That was his way.

And that is something that differs significantly from Nicola and I.

A LESSON IN BEING HERE

This is a real lesson in being in the moment. In the now.

Right now Peter Dooley is an old aged, immobile, disabled man.

That's what he is.

It's not helpful to get caught up in what he was.

The important point is to be here with him as he is now in this moment at this time.

If you get caught in the past and what somebody was then you will miss what they are now and what their needs are now.

It is a big lesson in being here in this very moment now.

When we are fully present right here in this moment we are able to do what needs to be done now and we are alive to the needs of this moment.

SUNDAY 8 DECEMBER

Sleeping - eyelids flickering.

Grumbly cough.

Takes a few spoonfuls of thickened water.

Wincing look on face.

Gurgly throat and cough.

4th day in a row no breakfast.

That gurgle is pretty bad.

Trying hard to cough and shift that phlegm but very weak and the stuff stays sitting there and the gurgling continues.

Sober Christmas.

Doesn't look happy when dealing with that gurgly stuff and the weakened attempt to clear it in vain.

Very bad gurgly.

Nurse Maria comes and looks at him.

They'll slide him back up towards the bed head and elevate him and hopefully that'll help drain the fluid that's accumulated over night.

Nurse Maria comes to give him his medication.

We play Mozart for him and spoon him porridge following the meds to help remove the taste of the meds.

Arrange for a nurse to feed him and read to him poetry including John O'Donohue and William Stafford.

SUNDAY 8 DECEMBER: MUSING TO MY BROTHERS ON DAD'S CONDITION, AND OUR JOURNEY TOWARD DYING

Ok, so I really didn't think Dad would still be with us now, and so, I'm writing the following based on the fact that all predictions have proved incorrect to date. Nicola, her friend Rheyse, and I are booked to fly to Perth on Tuesday 21 January for Cin's birthday, returning to Sydney on Sunday 26 January 2020 (Australia Day).

Who knows where things will be at vis-a-vis Dad as at 21 January, but based on the present track record I've thought it better to let you guys know now, so we can all plan accordingly.

He's certainly not well at the moment, and he could die within weeks, or he could continue, though not in a good state, for some time.

From my understanding a Glioblastoma diagnosis is a particularly difficult one to predict, and the patient can die faster than people had expected, or continue to suffer, but live within the illness for much longer than would be thought.

He certainly doesn't look or sound good, but he's still eating and drinking, and spits out one word answers to nurses, so who knows how long he has left.

In the end he ate his porridge and had his drink.

He slept at lunch and didn't have lunch.

Graham Price (Father of Ray Price) visited this arvo. He was happy to sit and pray for and with Dad. But Dad was sleeping the whole time.

But we had a good time Reading to him M Scott Peck's "Golf and the Spirit."

TUESDAY 10 DECEMBER 5:02AM

We are moving closer towards the time that dad will die.

It is not easy.

His body is continuing to deteriorate and parts of it are failing him.

This body that has been so strong and reliable for him for his whole life.

It is heart wrenchingly difficult.

He is going through it.

In "The Death of Ivan Ilyich" by Leo Tolstoy the dying man Ivan Ilyich only had his servant Gerasim to be there for him.

He is dying and he needs support.

And we will be there for him as much and as little as we can be.

As difficult as it is for us, it is more difficult for him.

He needs support, and we are supporting him, and we need support, and we are receiving support, and he is grateful and we are grateful.

We are coming closer to the end for Dad but not for life.

Nicola went to her year 10 school formal with Pat yesterday and life continues.

I will show Dad photos of Nicola at her year 10 Formal.

Today is Tuesday 10 December 2019 and my brother Matthew a.k.a. Chuck is arriving this coming Friday, 13 December 2019 so he will be with Dad from that day.

Dad will be grateful to have Chuck there as he has not been around for four months since approximately 10 August.

It's amazing how fast those four months have gone.

My older brother Phil has been following up Chuck and I to find out the dates when we will be with Dad, but he has not indicated anything about any time at all when he will be coming over.

I don't know if he will be coming over and seeing Dad again before Dad dies.

I don't know.

We don't know how much longer Dad has left.

I am driving through a smoke haze that makes it difficult to see clearly.

I just noticed a pedestrian emerge out of nothingness.

The sky is an apocalyptic grey with a tinge of burning.

It's forecast to be 41°C here today.

In a curious way it all seems related to the situation that Dad is in. As the fog and smog closes in the clarity diminishes, but the brightness of the lights becomes clearer.

Perhaps this is part of what Dad and we are experiencing as the clarity of daylight disappears behind a veil.

As the clarity of daylight disappears behind a veil of mist, the truth of the light becomes more evident and clear.

So let us continue to shine our light as best we can.

BLESSING FROM MARY ON TUESDAY 10 DECEMBER

Today as I walked through the breakfast dining area I met with the girl behind the counter whose name is Lovelein but everybody calls her Love.

And sitting across from Love's counter was Mary - her true name as well - she's mainly known as Queen Mary by her husband who calls themselves King David and Queen Mary.

And Mary was asking something in Arabic, and then I realised was asking how Dad is.

And I told her,

"Sleeping."

And she said in English,

"What can you do?"

And as I departed, she put her hand up in a blessing pose and said to me in English,

"Blessings to you."

So I got blessed by Mary this morning.

And then I take Mum shopping at Aldi and we have to arrange for Mum to take the checkout lady's chair to sit on before she collapses.

All of our items are processed and it's then that I realise that I've left my wallet in the car.

The guy immediately next to me says I'll pay for it.

With everything that's happening with Dad at the moment I nearly tear up and croak out a choked up, "Thank you so much. Merry Christmas."

The man's young son is just looking at him in bewilderment wondering why his dad would buy a stranger groceries.

Even when mum and I then relayed it back to the ladies at the nursing home I tear up again.

Mary, she has some blessing!

Returning that afternoon I end up spending more time with King David and Queen Mary.

Mary had suffered two strokes last week and has just returned from spending five days in hospital.

She has multiple brain tumours and suffers from seizures.

David greets me in the hallway and invites me in to see Mary in her room.

And I told them both the story of how she gave me the blessing in the morning, and then the man paid for my groceries at Aldi within hours of Mary giving me the blessing.

David and Mary were very pleased to hear of this.

David told me how Mary has spent most days of her life praying and talking to people about God.

They call me Solomon.

Apparently they believe that my name translates into Solomon in their Arabic language.

They kind of took me in as a son and told me how they had never been able to have children and that the name that they had always held in their hearts for a child was Solomon.

It was all very emotional and quite a significant experience for all of us.

Mary did not want to let go of my hand.

Still very touched by our moments together.

TUESDAY 10 DECEMBER

Sleeping peacefully.

Miriam says that she was told that Dad had a little bit of dinner last night.

Bit of a difficult cough there.

Nobody had tried to feed him or give him his meds by the time I had to go to Mum so I arranged for RN Louie to follow up Miriam for Dad's meds and to try to feed him porridge.

He ate a little bit of porridge and had some fluid.

Sleeping through lunch.

Pretty Sharma the level 2 Manager and RN Louie came and checked on him. And they couldn't rouse him so they left him.

Miriam says that Dad ate a bit for dinner last night.

WEDNESDAY 11 DECEMBER

Manager Jan comes in with me to check on him and he's sleeping soundly and looks comfortable and relaxed.

RN Jolie came and checked on him.

He didn't eat or take fluids last night. Which means he hasn't eaten since Monday.

We attempt to give him fluids and porridge twice but no response. RN Jolie does this.

It's at the stage where only the RN feeds him initially now, and if the RN approves food then others feed him.

Sleeping through wash and change by Kim and another nurse.

RN Jolie checks on him again.

More sleeping.

Jan and a guy who's an expert on repositioning to avoid pressure sores come and confirm he's in a good position.

Speak with RN Jolie and Level 2 Manager, Pretty Sharma, and they indicate that if he doesn't eat or drink again that his body will begin shutting down, and that may, or may not have already begun.

Peacefully sleeping with CDs playing pleasant music.

Lunch time still not stirring.

Jim and Pat Cunningham and B came in.

No food intake as at 1:40pm today, but took the tiniest smidgen of thickened water from B - 1/4 of a teaspoon.

He was communicating with B by drinking.

B left a bit before 2:30pm.

Client Liaison Kerry comes and checks on him.

As at 3pm no stirring or fluid or food intake today.

Dr B saw him last night and she is aware of his condition and will continue monitoring him and communicating with everybody.

The RNs come and check on Dad at change over.

The Probians visited: Ray, Ken Ward and Varis Preiss.

At 4:20pm he started shaking a bit and coughed for the first time today.

RN gave him a small .5mg Midazolam to reduce agitation.

But they are saying that not taking anything for 48 hours is of significant concern.

This is the first time that this has happened. In the past he's always bounced back to having a meal after missing 2 meals but this is now missing 5 meals and not really showing any indication of changing as at 4:40pm this arvo.

His lips didn't move when I left and tried to put fluid on them.

Reaching in, I hug him, and say, "I love you."

MESSAGE TO THE GOLDEN OLDIES CRICKETERS

Morning John, Darryl, Tony and Paul,

Dad continues to decline, so if you do want to see him please just make your way in.

No need to check with us beforehand but feel free to contact me or Matt.

Please pass this message on to others so they're up to date as well.

Wishing you all the best,

Simon

PS His Life Member Shirt maintains pride of place at the foot of his bed

NIGHT OF FRIDAY 13 DECEMBER – CHERRY HARMONY FESTIVAL STREET PARTY

And then tonight, Friday, 13 December, Sacha falls asleep in the car on the way home from the Friday night festivities of the Manjimup Cherry Harmony Festival. I lean over to pick her up and like a flash I remember the last time I was involved in this type of transaction was when Dad would lift me out of the car once we got home to Lapstone when I had fallen asleep in the car on the night drive home from Gran's or Nanna's, and I both thought of Sacha's tiny little body, in the same way that mine had been picked up and carried to bed by my father, and now as he lay in his last days in the Gracewood nursing home I was remembering how he had done what I was now doing, and I was deeply moved. Sacha's limp body, carried by me in the same way that mine had been carried by my father so many years ago but still so real within my experience.

And as I drive up the driveway and into the carport I say, *"Ok, Hazel, it's your time now."*

EARLY HOURS OF SATURDAY 14 DECEMBER

Awaking in the night
    Standing outside
    Encompassed by stars
    Thinking of those who have passed

SATURDAY 14 DECEMBER

Message from Chuck
   Dad has passed

SATURDAY 14 DECEMBER

Gran ("Hazel") was there for Dad
    Dad was there for me
    I am there for Dad
    Hazel was there for Dad

SATURDAY 14 DECEMBER - WE ARE NOW HAVING TO COME TO TERMS WITH THE NEW NORMAL

Dad has gone.

No more trips to the Gracewood to see Dad and to help him.

That time is over.

Things have been changing for some years now.

Dad has not been completely 100% for a while, and he has been dying for a number of years, and now he has died, and we are all having to come to terms with it, and it is not an easy thing to come to terms with.

Things will change.

Mum remains physically healthy, and it is presently unknown what the new family dynamics will be.

Dad has gone.

What does this mean for all of us?

It means different things to different people.

It's hard to grasp.

He was very proud of his three sons, and their partners, and his grandchildren.

He will be missed, as he missed them.

This last year has been a very difficult, challenging one as it has seen him in some sort of hospital care for the whole of the year.

2019 was Dad's year of being in the hospital.

He endured it.

He did not enjoy it.

Now he is released.

All sorts of questions arise about fathers and sons.

Dad was so loved and well respected by so many different people.

It's hard to comprehend.

DAD WAS ALWAYS STRONG AND HEALTHY - DIARY NOTE ON THE EVE OF DAD'S FUNERAL

Dad was always strong, and healthy, and struggled to understand my weaknesses with the allergy reactions that I've suffered from.

He tried to understand, but always having been so healthy and strong it was difficult for him to understand.

He loved me through it, but it was a cause of frustration for him that he could not fix it.

Just as it was a cause of frustration for him that he could not do anything to fix his wife Margaret's mental health condition.

He was a man of the people, and they loved him.

He was a Christian, like those Christians, and they loved him.

Now he's gone.

Gone.

And we all feel it.

Nor did he understand my artistic temperaments and tendencies.

He encouraged me to do law instead of pursuing acting.

He made a big fuss about a series of photos that I took of a leaf that I was enamoured by down in the bush, that I was trying to photograph with the perfect light.

He tried his best and that is all you can ask of anybody.

It is a difficult thing to have somebody go.

Mum says, "I have to go Simon," when I raise something about the funeral.

Few others have been in contact with Mum.

I find this very sad and disturbing and it upsets me greatly.

Somebody with mental illness is certainly not going to go well with being completely ostracised, and ignored, and unloved by their family.

Dad used to pay Z to be this sort of paid friend for Mum.

All of this is very strange and confusing.

All this stuff would've been water off a duck's back for Dad but he was him, and I am who I am.

I don't know how it was really for my parents when their parents passed.

Just like most things in my family we never talked about it.

And that is one of my regrets.

I do feel tired and I have a sore back and I'm somewhat trepidatious about tomorrow.

SATURDAY 21 DECEMBER

Visit Jim the Roseman, and Pat in the morning and Jim the Roseman talks like a maniac, but somehow he speaks sense that I understand and take on board.

Jim the Roseman tells me I'm passed my prime, which inspires me all the more to go for my walk, but I can't go for my walk because this man will not come for a walk with me, because he doesn't believe in walking.

"Okay right now because I believe I can do this walk."

That line was Jim the Roseman speaking nonsense and that's why it doesn't make any sense.

He is Jim the Roseman not Jim the rosemary.

MUM

Mum is not going well at all.

She said, "I'm not feeling very well within myself."

SUNDAY 22 DECEMBER

Mum has been in the foyer waiting for Brian and Bobbie Houston to come. "Oh Sime, I'm so let down."

Mum thinks the memorial service for Dad will be lovely.

In chatting with Mum she prayed that she just wants to go home to heaven.

CHRISTMAS EVE

Following on from our discussion last night, it's interesting, I notice how ready I am to go into a righteous anger/rage, but not sadness and loss.

A CHRISTMAS BLESSING, KIND OF

So if another of your family members died?

How would you respond?

This is a great question for unlocking compassion.

It's also a great question for asking questions about family and relationships.

My brother has been more a part of his group of people than our family since he was a teenager.

And yet there are familial obligations and there is Dooley family history.

Presuming that everybody does the best that they can and that he does the best that he can then there is room for care and compassion toward him and his family.

It is not just all about me.

This is an important truth to always bear in mind and remember.

So something that you have to comprehend, and understand, is that there is a great likelihood of a tragedy befalling another family member.

And you will have not wanted to have done anything yourself to cause harm, or upset, now, or before, or during, that time.

When the tragedy arises you have to be ready then.

You can't be trying to get up to speed in the moment.

Do the work now.

Unlock compassion within yourself now.

Think about how hard it is for you with the loss of Pa now.

Use active imagination to consider the situation, and circumstances of the tragic death of a much younger person in difficult circumstances.

Study the work of the greats:

Nelson Mandela

Martin Luther King

Mohandas Mahatma Gandhi

Shakyamuni Siddhartha Buddha

As Stephen Jenkinson talks about, death is the overwhelming deity that must be respected and that we must come to seek reconciliation with.

Death is taboo within our culture, but a shift is occurring, and you are a part of it.

So create, and imagine a created reality, with your family on your side of the equation.

I understand that it is a work of your active imagination, done in order to benefit, and foster goodwill, and health within yourself and your family.

As Michael and Ann Barbato, and Judith, of the Midwifing Dying Course pointed out to you, the raw unvarnished truth is most often too hard for a person to accept.

This is why people like X and also Y live in a fantasyland in which they inhabit.

But there are elements to existence that fall within Françoise O'Kane's book Dark Chaos.

Read and study Dark Chaos and learn how to inhabit this world that incorporates dark chaos within it.

Continue to develop, and maintain, your boundaries, and choose who you deal with and who you respond to.

But don't get addicted to righteous indignation, and the intoxication of being right.

Be cool Dools.

Relax.

Chill.

It's no big deal.

Love, and open yourself up to love.

Love your way.

Allow people to come to you.

Continue to prepare to be there when the tragedy strikes, and:

– eliminates theology, and doctrinal differences.

Remember the lady that looks like Nanna who turned up at Nanna's funeral.

A lady who had been cast out of Nannas sphere, and yet she arrived.

It is time for you to work on your benign indifference, and your capacity for compassionate being.

Call on Ram Dass.

Engage in active imagination about what you, and Cin, would do if a tragedy befell either of your brother's families.

Consider the stories we might share.

Consider again how to be a healing presence.

Consider how to let bygones be bygones.

Find your space and your way.

You have nothing to prove.

You are simply living your life your way.

Simply be.

Love.

Allow your higher Self, and guides to be there with you and those who need support.

You have nothing to prove.

Let it go.

Feel compassion for those who are not free of dogma and theology, and all of those ideas that can hold a person.

NO DAD CHRISTMAS

Dad's passing is a harbinger of change.

It is a stark reminder that we will all go.

Although it is slow, and gradual, and we lose contact with people.

Yes we all go.

Most don't die suddenly in their younger years, but rather, slowly, gradually fade away, and live out their final period beneath the shadows of a retirement village or nursing home.

That was the case for Nicola's Grandpa, and for my Dad, Nicola's Pa.

. . .

It is difficult to cope with and to come to terms with Dad's passing.

BOXING DAY

I weep for the 12-year-old Margaret Archer at Warragamba.

She was the school captain of Warragamba Public School.

She suffered so much.

And I wonder what was it that created the creature that became, and was, Laurel Mavis Archer, and what she did to her daughter.

FRIDAY 27 DECEMBER XPT

One week since Dad's funeral.

I can't believe the week has gone so fast.

I hosted 4 Couchsurfers last night.

Marion and Linnea from Norway.

And Julien and Lorene from France.

Fun night with aperitif out on the back balcony.

7:14am Depart Hornsby Station on the XPT.

Some confusing dreams involving something to do with Dad last night.

Fully booked service on the XPT. Lucky I got a seat.

Broadmeadow at 9:36am.

Our family drove up the F3, as it was called then, so many times on our way to visit Dad's Mum, Hazel Dooley aka Gran in Raymond Terrace, Terrigal.

The red tinged Christmas Bush is out.

We must be open to different ways of thinking and being.

There's a lot to work through re Dad's passing.

Arriving in Gosford, and remembering driving through the winding bends in and out of Gosford to visit Gran in Terrigal, and being afraid of foxes, and falling asleep as we drove through the dark with just the headlights to see.

The other day, the person I was with asked us a lot of questions when we were together but we didn't really talk about how were feeling about Dad's passing, and our memories and grief, and related feelings and emotions.

People vibrate at different frequencies and we do well to accept this.

The funeral was this time last week...

...a lot to go through...

Today is Friday 27 December and we have the Memorial Service at QH at 2pm Monday 30 December.

When someone dies so much goes with them.

So much.

So much shared.

Now lost.

It's hard.

And it must be terribly difficult for her.

MONDAY 30 DECEMBER

Dream of seeing airplanes fighting in the sky.

Then I see a missile lit up and coming toward our building in the city.

And Cin and I are unpacking in a hurry.

And an annoying man comes and addresses me abruptly and steps on my left foot and I direct him to get out and I grab him and send him away.

4:20am alarm where I'm sleeping in Remy's room.

I'd awoken twice in the night and need to pee now.

A mozzie has kept disturbing me and waking me all morning.

4:30am drop off.

5:10am the bus still hasn't arrived.

Bus over half an hour late.

Bus driver laughs at idea of getting me to the airport to catch the plane on time.

Jayne coming to take me.

5:20am the loudest street sweeping truck comes by and nearly blows all my luggage away.

Ph 132232 but only open from 7am to 10pm for refund.

I go to fill my water bottle at the park.

Somebody lying on a bench in the Brunswick Heads community shed sleeping. A Backpackers van is parked with its sliding door slightly open.

Jayne drives me to Coolangatta Gold Coast Airport with just enough time to check bag, pass slow security checkpoint, get explosives scanned, walk airport, fill water bottle, toilet, order muffin, collect muffin, join queue, pass ticketing, walk to back stairs and board plane to seat 28f up the back with a whole row of 3 seats to myself.

Take off.
Remember 20 yrs ago with Carolyn up here.
For the Y2K.
We'd stayed at Carolyn's friend Michael's parents place.
The dad was Pete the retired fireman.
Afterwards Carolyn and I stayed at the foot of Wollumbin/Mt Warning in a peaceful jacaranda filled caravan park.
I'm filled with such sadness and regret at the passing of the years and all that has gone.

Brown blotches among green, like camo outfit. From where the bushfires were.

Big day today.

The Memorial Service for Dad at 2pm at Mum's Quakers Hill Nursing Home.

Flying back at such great speed compared to the long, slow trip up by train and car.

My cousin smokes a hell of a lot.

I imagine she continues to carry with her much emotional pain, probably especially the loss of her Mum in such difficult circumstances.

Very brown bush below from bushfires and a stretch of smoke still coming up where fire continues.

8am fly over Bondi Beach, it's crescent shape facing South East.

Striations of bushfire smoke over Sydney.

Very smoggy.

We fly out for miles over the blue wrinkled ocean, white caps fascinating my eye, the fun of the plane on a steep bank giving me a great window view straight down like look through a glass bottom boat, which reminds me of our trips to Fiji and Vanuatu when Dad still had so much life ahead of him in this life/that life.

Another plane is a small dot out there circling the same far, wide flight path we're on, as we feel the bump of the landing gear dropping.

Cabin crew be seated for landing.

And the Dooleybird is coming in.

Orange bushfire sun reflected on the crinkled, iridescent ocean.

Over the top of a small tinny with 3 fishermen.

Ground rush speed.

Wing flaps up.

Reverse thrust.

Forces pressing forward and then the easy:

"Welcome to Sydney where the local time is 11 minutes past 8"

And that little, fun, healing North Coast adventure has been concluded.

Now for the Memorial Service afternoon at Nanny's...

AND DOWN THIS ROAD I GO JUST LIKE MY FATHER BEFORE ME

On the last day of the year. On the last day of the last year that Dad was with us.

I drive down the road that he drove down so many times, and we drove down so many times together.

It is a coincidence.

I am driving to visit my friends who have invited me to see them for New Year's Eve.

But nevertheless, I am driving down the road that Dad drove down for so many decades, and I am driving down this road on the last day, of the last year of the last decade, that he was with us.

At the beginning of this decade he was still driving down this road to work, and now he is gone from the body that we knew him in.

And there is a loss, and the grief that comes with that.

It is a loss, and a grief, that is incomprehensible and cannot be put into words.

And driving down this road now, as I drive I am filled with sadness, and regret, and longing, and words incapable of being found and spoken.

And I drive down this road because I must drive down this road, because I have no other option but to drive down this road.

And down this road I go.

Just like my father before me.

And I am filled with missing, and wondering where the years went, and what I'm doing, and what all this means.

And there are fires blazing like a ring around the city, and like a ring around this nation, and like a ring around this island.

And I'm sad.

Those times are the times we had.

NEW YEAR'S

This time three years ago she, and Peter celebrated NYE together.

They didn't know he had the GBM.

They didn't know they were celebrating the year he'd be diagnosed.

Confronting stuff.

They didn't know.

Oblivious.

Obliviously happy.

What to say???

ON THE EVE OF MY FIRST BIRTHDAY WITHOUT YOU

When someone dies that is that.

They are gone from that body and that is the end of that.

There is no more opportunity to do things together, or to ask them questions about things in their life in this life.

It is a resounding silence.

The feeling that remains after the sound of the gong has ended.

Remembering Dad.

BLACK WALLABY

Thich Nhat Hanh talks about how when people are hurting their pain spills over into you.

I meant to write onto but maybe into is more apt.

My friend A revealed for the first time yesterday that he is no longer actively pursuing his long term business idea.

This is a soul loss that he has not grieved, and is suffering, and is causing him pain.

He was so unhappy.

Things are changing.

I just saw, and in particular, heard the Black Wallaby crunching through the bush here in the north east section of the Glenhaven Valley.

A talks a big game but he is suffering a loss, and he has a lot of undealt with issues, and as I said before I am not his therapist so the nature of our engagement is going to change.

It is the same with B.

B is on a holiday with friends and we have not had any real contact at all.

Things are changing, and things have changed, and I am no longer chasing.

I am no longer chasing.

I am the Black Wallaby doing my thing and being quite content.

I have my work to do, and I will play a mind game where I place a pretend monetary value on each hour of the time I spend engaging in an activity that is not humming, and synchronous, and a part of my soul journey, and soul expression.

As a result of this I will be happier, and more content, and less critical, and easier to get on with, and more loving, and these are great reasons for no longer chasing old relationships with people who aren't loving, and wanting, to engage with me.

Like that old dry piece of bark I just saw falling off that tree, it is a graceful letting go, and simply being with my experience.

I don't chase.

And I do my work.

I am, and have, soul friends.

And you move on in gratitude, for what is, and what has been.

It's important to remember that A and B are not practising artists, and so there's only so much they can relate to you on - remember this. It'll help you understand them and yourself - just like your interactions with your Dad who was not a practising artist but was, rather, a professional man like A and B.

A, like all current culture city dwellers is entirely enmeshed in the Apollonian Matrix. And the Dionysian balance to that does not receive any look in at all. But I am engaging the Dionysian balance and so we don't harmonise because we're vibrating on different frequencies and attracted to different ways of being.

GO TO WHERE THE LOVE IS

By not chasing people I am only engaging in a subtle shift. My friendliness towards people continues. It is just that I am no longer chasing them and taking significant time out of my day to meet them where they want to meet me and to accommodate them and their special needs. I am living independently and according to my own schedule, and needs, and work obligations, and activities, and the requirements of my health, well-being, recreation and soul needs schedule. All of this is based on my needs, as in non-violent communication NVC. So it's nothing against the people that I am no longer chasing or seeing. If the outcome of my no longer chasing is that we no longer see each other, then it becomes clear that it was a one-sided, and therefore, unhealthy relationship because I was chasing them. Obviously the situation with Mum is different, because of the nature of her condition, causing her to be rendered so passive. It's important for me to understand that these are simply changes in life and that there is nothing to be personally offended in it for either myself or my friends. I have done my hard work and in pursuing/chasing them have potentially set up unbalanced relationships. I have the things that I want to do, and they have the things that they want to do, and if we happen to coalesce then that is fine, but if we don't then that is the way that it is, and that is okay too.

Generate love.

Go to where the love is.

A and B and I have all helped each other at times of need, however, perhaps we are not in those times of needing each other at the moment and so we are off on our separate hero's journeys, each making our way into the forest at the point where it is darkest and there is no path.

Questions to ask of yourself and the people you engage with:

What are you enlivened by?

What is enlivening you?

Think of other questions of a similar nature.

Use these questions to stir yourself up.

Also use the questions with friends.

It will help you, and the friends, to discover whether it's worth spending time together.

Don't over strain yourself, or try too hard with things. Breathe and simply allow yourself to do what you are doing. And allow other cares and concerns to pass.

Listen to audiobooks and music.

Ask Questions of yourself:

What are you enlivened by?

What is enlivening you?

LETTER TO A FRIEND

Thank you dear,

I am writing to you from my father's house in Sydney. It's impossible to comprehend that he has gone - it is just so unreal/surreal. But that time has ended. Gone. I've been going through old Christmas, Birthday and Get Well cards of Dad's today, and the emotion welling up was tangible and uncomfortable.

But, being here in his house day after day does help tremendously with coming to terms with his passing. And such a mix of feelings and emotions, but an overwhelming sadness, and at times a gut ache.

On the last day that I saw Dad before he passed I received my Certificate of Completion of the Midwifing Dying Course. It was like a message from Mystery informing me, "You've done all you could Son. You're graduating today." Very bittersweet.

I've read a lot of Stephen Jenkinson's work about grieving, and he speaks of the fear of forgetting, and the guilt of enjoying yourself. And that we need to overcome these fears, and feelings of guilt. For, as you say, they want us to live, and to feel, and to experience joy. I am so pleased to hear that you had this joyful moment today.

I've been safe from bushfires the whole time, but am well aware of what's going on, and feel powerless within it. Here's a recent note: "Thursday 2 January

The bushfire smoke awoke me in the early morning

It's so thick and bad that it's unhealthy to walk outside this morning"

You asked how my New Year's was. I was very fortunate to be invited for dinner by friends. But, even going to their place was full of more strangeness because to get to their place I had to drive along the same road that Dad had driven to work for decades, and this was now the end of the last decade that he'd done that. And I never drive that road so it was a very poignant experience. But, again, though it was hugely emotional, it was ultimately a beautiful, cathartic experience, and it was so poetic to be doing that on the last day of the decade. And on New Year's Day I took Nicola and her friend to a beach pool and I baptised myself in the water for the new year and it felt wonderful, and refreshing, and I closed my eyes and floated, weightless, supported, buoyant on the saltwater.

Saturday was my first birthday since Dad's passing and that was weird. Looking to see him, but he's not there. Going to phone him, and a split second later remembering he's passed. He was so reliable and he would always be at my birthday, and doing something special for me. It's a hell of a thing. It was a good day with my loving daughter, Nicola and friends. And Nicola wrote me the most beautiful, tear-producing card. But, there was something about the day that was just not right, and that feeling remains.

Though, yesterday morning I was allured along a path in the bush and came upon the elusive black wallaby, and that felt special and encouraging.

Your cooling vibes have worked magic and it's just rained properly here for the first time in months!

I value our friendship greatly and am always supported, and encouraged by you. With love, gratitude, and much warmth, I remain,

Simon

POSTING A LETTER TO A FRIEND - ONE MONTH SINCE

I took your advice and have walked through the bush and up to the mailbox to post this letter to you. It is a strange and lonely existence living here in this empty house where nobody ever visits. I think of the lonely times Dad must've had here and think how he must've wondered how, after everything his life had to come to this - living alone in Margaret's "dream house" down the bottom of a long private road, without any family, or company to speak of. It was not a time of peaceful tranquility and reflection. It was a time when a man who had been extroverted and engaged his whole life found himself in a forced solitude without any opportunity for change. I can see why he went to America to be with Chuck and Jenny and the family that had lived with him, and had moved there. The ideology of the church had internalised this forced isolation on him (and her). And it was an insurmountable prison with enforcers who would never allow them to live their basic happiness of togetherness.

. . .

I was thinking back to September and how my mood was different then.

Although Dad had terminal cancer in September he was still alive.

And there is an unspeakable difference between the time when the person is dying, and the time afterwards when they are gone.

DYING

Hi hun,

Weakened, I stumble from the shower, grasping the towels in my next to final act. That act is to grab the bin.

I fall onto the bed, water everywhere. I'm lying in my own pool of shower water, but I cannot move. My head is a sodden, lead weight bowling ball in the pillow.

Except, as I soon learn, I still have the capacity to lean over to my right and throw up, repeatedly, into the bin, thinking that I've just lost the medication I took, but also contemplating how you often feel better after throwing up.

And there I lay until afternoon, racing through our multiverses at light speed, with tangible pauses.

. . .

I'm dying. I've died. I'm dying. I've died.

Until, eyes open upon a new scenario. The smoke lifting, I'm beginning to see clearly, though my body remains, barely able to carry me. I wonder how long this feeling will last. And I resolve to at least try for shower round 2 and hopefully a different outcome. And that is where I'm at as I write this to you. I hope you're faring considerably better :)

x

"SPELLING"

Stephen Jenkinson is really onto something with the importance of words,
and really delving into words and meaning,
and the casting of "spells" with spelling,
and the uncasting of "spells" with spelling.

We are casting "spells" all the time.
So, let us court wisdom (Sophia the Greek Goddess of wisdom).
Let us be lovers/friends of wisdom - Philo-Sophia,
and speak in ways that mindfully cast spells from the place/s of love.

TRANSITION-ING

This has been a time of transition.

It has been a time of ups and downs.

Dad's funeral was a coming together of people within a sphere of love.

It was like the blue glowing orb that Dad had seen where the people were being put into.

There have been many lonely times and in many ways it has been a challenging and uneasy month.

However there was the healing road trip with Joshua Tree Thomason.

And then again a return to Newcastle where Paul Iannuzzelli and I put down the first two tracks of Tenders of the Lost Field for The Story of Things Unspoken.

I have not spent as much time with Nicola as I would have liked nor has Nicola stayed over as much as I would've liked.

Nicola has hardly stayed over at all and we have not done a Jervis trip.

Nicola is busier than ever with her work at the Dural IGA, and with time spent at home, and with friends, and with her boyfriend Pat.

I am finding my own way slowly and with much pain.

My friends and I have hardly had any contact since my birthday on 4 January.

There have been some very special moments with Nicola like when she drove me to the Thai restaurant at Pennant Hills for my birthday.

And when we went on our trip together to Palm Beach.

Just the two of us.

Another very special moment.

I love her more than words can say and fortunately, unlike so many, this has been able to be conveyed.

Cin is extremely supportive and encouraging in all of my creative endeavours.

I am a very fortunate man indeed.

REVISITING THE GRACEWOOD ON MONDAY 20 JANUARY

Mary and David in the Gracewood blessed me.

Mary kissed me.

And David hugged me and told me he loved me.

And David told me that his heart goes with me.

It was a beautiful moment with them.

On my visit to the Gracewood a month after Dad has passed.

WALKING IN THE HEAT

I'm walking in the heat, and I'm actually getting something out of the heat, and the sweat, and I'm remembering how I walked in this heat, in the sweat, and grieved Dad's illness when he flew back in from America, this time, this day, one year ago, and this was when the first of my big grieving really happened, and it was intense, and it was terrible, and it was a loss, and it was hard, and it was healing, and it was tremendous, and this was where it all began, as I walked in that giant Mexican hat from Castle Hill to the house at Glenhaven, and I went and I listened to Lady Gaga's dedicated song to her grandfather on the Edge of Glory, for him as he lay dying.

And even now I remember that, and I remember Dad, and I remember...
    ...and I remember.

I remember you.

LETTER TO A FRIEND 6 WEEKS AFTER HIS PASSING

I walked the complete length of the beach yesterday from the southern end right up to that North Bondi grassy knoll, and as I stood there I thought about Dad, and how different we are. The way that he plodded along in the course of his career and marriage in ways that I could not. And I wished that I had been born to be more like that, rather than the peripatetic wanderer that I am. And wonderer for that matter. And I was filled with great sadness and a longing for a simple, contentment that in his own way Dad had. Think of, for instance, the particular songs that he chose for his funeral.

In short I am not Peter Dooley. I honoured him as best I could. But I suppose one way to consider my present way of being is that I am subject to a violent, swinging pendulum.

I'm reminded of the myth of Parzifal/Parcifal/Percival, the one who pierced the veil. If you explore this myth you will see a lot of my story in it.

With my recent interest in hiking/camping and related wild

elements I can feel the South arising and the Wild Indigenous One. And obviously the encounters with Michael Meade, Stephen Jenkinson and Bill Plotkin himself indicate a slow and gradual journey toward what I am becoming. There has certainly been ground work there in those realms.

And I'm feeling called on more heroes journeys within my hero's journey. True, there is the Castle Parzifal found, but he did not stay there without going out and back on many more adventures, after his initial arrival. He continued to go a-venturing, sometimes wisely, sometimes foolishly, but going as his heart directed.

And, yes, that song does speak to me so well:

"I wish there was a treaty we could sign."

This came to be my grieving song for Dad as I wished there was a treaty we could sign between life and death itself. And, like most elements of grief a gift comes from it, and that gift is the understanding that I wish there could be a treaty between so many competing tensions. I wish there could be a treaty within my own tension between a Peter Dooley styled plodding contentment and my own restlessness, yearnings, and what could well appear to others to be nonsensical, and ridiculous ways.

I am drawn to continue exploring. There is much pain, and loss, and something else that perhaps I will know its name later. In my own way, as a child, I had my own form of contentment in the Blue Mountains. I can remember sitting alone on my bike on the side of the steep slope looking all around me as a boy of Jasper's age and asking with a great wrenching sorrow in my heart, *"Why would anyone ever want to leave this place?"*

And since that time, when I was just 13 I have not felt as home as I do now. And, having left in 1986 I will be returning to that place and to those people in the Blue Mountains for the first time in the middle of this year, for the Blaxland High School reunion, and I am full of trepidation.

My body actually had a violent allergic reaction to the move down from the Blue Mountains. If it were not for modern medicine it would've killed me. Sydney sits within a deep geographical basin that collects and contains all of the atmospheric muck. My body reacted to this by having my first ever asthma attack. Dad stayed up through the whole night and kept me alive.

The doctors said that the only way that I would be cured would be to move west of the Blue Mountains into a drier setting. It was a mismatch between my body and the Sydney Basin. I always wanted to get out of Sydney and as I was nearing the end of my undergraduate law studies I was planning to go and do further studies and legal practice in either the UK or America, but the devil's own emissary in the form of a lawyer gave me an offer I couldn't refuse to come and be his protégé. My artistic dreams had been long submerged by then. But one thing I remember very clearly is sitting with this lawyer, who was a particularly friendly emissary of the devil, as many of them are, and saying to him, *"I can't just stay and work in Sydney for my whole life."*

But I kept burrowing deeper and deeper into an embedded life in Sydney and it took a hell of a lot for Mystery to extract me. The irony of course being that I write this to you from deep inside the Sydney Basin.

I have penned many a song of the heart to you, and this is yet another.

What may sound surprising as being one of the most challenging parts of last year's caring for Dad was the fact that I could not get in and out from seeing Dad up there on the first floor without having to pass and greet between 8 to 30 people on the way in and on the way out, every time. Now for a Peter Dooley type that might have been wonderful. But, I like to come in and go quietly and privately as I please. In writing this I realise what a public life I lived until I travelled. I miraculously disappeared from my public life in Sydney and lived a quieter existence. This may seem paradoxical with performing and putting material out into the world. But that is not what I'm talking about. What I am talking about is living within a fishbowl setting where you are always involved with people in your immediate surroundings. Obviously you have this in school and it is inescapable there. But in church and most office and related environments it is an integral part of it. You are demanded to have few boundaries. I'm discovering what I'm saying as this writing occurs, and it is only happening because I am walking in the bush, alone, deep in the valley.

I'm all about Soul. And Soul and Mystery dance. And there is a welling from the deep that is powerful and dangerous and alluring. My dinner host from last night survived the tsunami. On our first night in the Perup with Bill Plotkin you and I are standing out on the ledge of a high jetty, jutting far out into the ocean, a huge wave, city-sized, rushes up before us, and crashes down, swamping us.

We remain standing, while the waters come up from the depths and down upon us.

We remain standing.

Remember this.

Remember this.

Remember this, this year.

And remember this in the coming years.

Love,

Sime

I HAVEN'T DONE THE FLIGHT OUT OF SYDNEY WHEN DAD HASN'T BEEN ALIVE

I haven't done the flight out of Sydney when Dad hasn't been alive in that body

In our dreams we find each other

What if all these metaphors are deceptive and there's just as much for us in the dark and the light, and it's irrelevant

In Dark Chaos Francoise O'Kane speaks of people who don't take the hero way but just surrender and give up all control

In our culture they may be labelled victims but they are not that

They are helped by others

DRAGONFLY ZEN

A dragonfly comes into the car from outside and rests on my pen

Zen – live Zen

Try without trying

The Tao

Relax and breathe

Release expectations

. . .

Increase your true aesthetic experiences and enjoyment

No more racing around, chasing – Be

Image of heart with taurus coming out of it in an ellipsis

Live out of your own centre of love

Be free to feel fear and acknowledge it and let it go

THIS

This is life

There is nothing more important than this to me

Soul journey and exploration is integral

Each of us is given to our own endeavours

For instance I am grateful to all of the people who cared for Dad over the course of his need for care

Hallelujah is an exhortation to give praise to Mystery for Being regardless of any present circumstances

. . .

I am
   A willing participant in the glory of existence

WRITING THIS

I've just been re-living for the first time the day when Dad transitioned

I've been reading through my notes from Dad's dying time and I just got to the moment of death

I didn't realise the state that I was in until I was in Woolworths and I just couldn't think or concentrate on anything clearly

I really feel like I am trying to operate in this world as an inhabitant of another

FLYING TO PERTH ON 10 MARCH 2020, JUST BEFORE THE COVID-19 CORONAVIRUS TRAVEL BAN

Remembering his favourite place

Oh God

Looking out the window at Jervis Bay and seeing Plantation Point

And knowing that Dad's not there

And that he's died

God it's soooooooooo hard

. . .

Remembering how much he just loved going there

And how much he loved that place

God

The golfers

The dog walkers

His "place"

So hard

So unbelievably difficult

If I hadn't done everything I absolutely possibly could've I'd be feeling even worse now

As it is I feel bad enough

As Jervis Bay recedes into the mist and beneath the incoming clouds

. . .

Beneath me is scorched earth

All blackened and bare from the intense bushfires

A moonscape

8 FEBRUARY 2019 DAD SPEAKING, UNDER A BLUE SKY, FROM HIS WHEELCHAIR, TO A VOLUNTEER LADY AT THE SAN CANCER HEALING GARDEN JUST BEFORE HIS THIRD AND FINAL OPERATION

"Yes, I used to be once like that gentleman, just being able to walk through here at my leisure, but you realise that times in your life come...

...I like it out in the sun.

At the moment I'm enjoying the sun, and I've got a coffee coming.

It's a very relaxing area, with the trees and all that.

Yep. So anyway, I'm very grateful for all those who are supporting me."

LIFE SPEAKING

As I walked this morning I was overwhelmed with thinking of Dad, and the tragedy of his final days. My legs felt as though they'd stumble, needing support, I reached for the closest tree and held it, finding some relief. The bark, it crumpled, fell. An ant walked past my hand, and then I saw a smaller one going on its path. The tree bark glistened golden, with a speck of green. And in my resting, a golden budgerigar flew down, rested on a branch, and then I heard the sound, a symphony of bird song. Feeling warmth upon the back of my legs, the morning sun at work, I thanked the tree, the birds, the sun. And one more touch upon this cool, firm trunk, before stepping back, I listen to the rustling leaves as they speak of great tragedy, and loss, and all around I'm told this is all the work of love. A zephyr, cooling my face, Sun's heating the back of my neck, bird's shadows passing. Slowly, now very slowly stepping into the golden path, walking soft in present memory, he's still gone, but life speaks love.

THANK YOU

Thank you for seeing this journey through with us. My prayer is that through our sharing of our grief, and loss, and love, we all may receive something of a blessing. I know I have.

In gratitude,

SJP Dooley

ABOUT THE AUTHOR

SJP Dooley is a writer, voice artist, actor, photographer, & co-founder of Stellar Violets Life Library Living Museum & Gallery. Through these, and other avenues, he seeks to give voice to soul, and engage with what it means to be present on this earth at this time. Inside Out Heart emerged from the struggle that was the final chapter of his father's life.

Volumes 1 & 2 Collection

Ebook ISBN: 978-1-922399-07-6

Paperback ISBN: 978-1-922399-06-9

Audiobook ISBN: 978-1-922399-08-3

www.stellarviolets.org

facebook.com/simon.dooley
twitter.com/simondooley
instagram.com/SJPDooley

ALSO BY SJP DOOLEY

Inside Out Heart Volume 1: Poems for my dying father & after

Inside Out Heart Volume 2: Diary notes of being with my dying father

Inside Out Heart spoken word poetry to music by SJP Dooley & Paul Avanti Iannuzzelli

www.ingramcontent.com/pod-product-compliance
Lightning Source LLC
Chambersburg PA
CBHW071724080526
44588CB00013B/1882